GREAT MARQUES
BMW

GREAT MARQUES
BMW

JEREMY WALTON

GENERAL EDITOR
JOHN BLUNSDEN

Cathay Books

CONTENTS

First published in Great Britain in 1983 by
Octopus Books Limited

This edition published in 1989 by
Cathay Books
Michelin House
81 Fulham Road
London SW3 6RB

ISBN 0 86178 570 3

Produced by Mandarin Offset
Printed and bound in Hong Kong

Author's note

I would like to thank Michael Schimpke, Paul Rosche and Diater Stappett of BMW Munich, and former BMW Competitions Manager Jochen Neerpasch, for their help and assistance by providing valuable information for the book. Thanks are also due to Klaus Wesner, Johannes Schultz and Richard Gerstner of the public relations department at BMW: Olaf von Gostowski and Hans Fleischmann of the BMW archives department; Raymond Playfoot, public relations manager, BMW (GB) Ltd Peter Samuelson of the BMW Car Club of Great Britain; and Wolfgang Marx of the International Council of BMW Clubs.

Jeremy Walton

All cars unless otherwise stated in the captions were kindly provided by BMW AG or BMW (GB) Ltd. Owners and custodians of the other cars, at the time of photography, are mentioned in the captions to the illustrations.

Special photography: **Ralner Schlegeimlich** and **Ian Dawson**

ENDPAPERS *Monaco, May 1980, with the multi-million dollar BMW M1 racing series in full cry.*

PAGES 1–5 *The 1982 BMW 635 CSi.*

SCATTERED ORIGINS

When the Bayerische Motoren Werke (BMW) began car manufacture in 1928 there were 25 marques of German origin on the home market. Today only seven survive. Yet among these seven marques are some of the world's most successful and prestigious car makers, a testament to a tenacious industry that has emerged successfully from two world wars and their economic aftermath. How BMW survived at various stages in its history through such diverse activities as aircraft engine manufacture and the production of aluminium cooking utensils is a story worth telling in its own right. Survival might have been thought enough, but BMW in the 1980s ranks alongside Porsche and Mercedes-Benz as the epitome of German quality-conscious car engineering. Of course motorcycles, based on the original flat twin-cylinder engine design of the 1920s, have been an integral part of BMW's advance to international respect, but this book concentrates primarily on the company's four-wheeled achievements. Indeed, the motorcycles are important enough to justify separate treatment—a comment that applies with equal force to BMW aero engine manufacture.

Tracing the foundation of the name BMW is a relatively straightforward task, for it was registered as Bayerische Motoren Werke GmbH ('Bavarian Motor Works') on 20 July 1917. But prior to this registration there had been a number of earlier mergers and companies that were all concerned with aero engine manufacture in the south German city of Munich. Also, to discover the origins of the car manufacturing side of BMW it is necessary to look back before the turn of the century to another company and to a base that is now firmly behind the Iron Curtain.

East German pioneers
BMW's first involvement in automobile manufacture can be dated to 3 December 1896. This date marks the foundation of a vehicle manufacturing company at Eisenach. Now in the German Democratic Republic, Eisenach was the original headquarters for all BMW car-building activity between 1928 and 1939; the inevitable wartime production then occupied the period until 1945 and the Allied invasion.

A castle above the town of Eisenach gave the new vehicle assembly company an emblem and a name under which to sell its munitions wagons and bicycles. The name was Wartburg, a marque familiar in Britain until the development of emission regulations in Western Europe prevented its two-stroke saloons from further sale in the United Kingdom.

The first Wartburg cars were made in 1898. After a period of experimentation with its own three- and four-wheel prototypes, the Eisenach factory entered into a manufacturing agreement on 12 September 1898 with the French light car makers Decauville. The Wartburg badge would adorn a 3½ hp two-cylinder design of 500 cc. Alternatively, an engine of 750 cc and 5 hp could be supplied. Both models had a disturbing open chain-drive transmission beneath the driver's seat. These cars appeared to be simply motorized versions of horse-drawn vehicles, but it should be remembered that the type of front suspension they employed—complete with transverse spring for the axle—was widely used by many mass production manufacturers up to 50 years later. However, the back axle had no suspension at all, ensuring that the occupants paid painful attention to every detail of their chugging progress.

History records that Wartburg was widely esteemed for its car, cycle and truck building activities during this period. BMW owners today will not be surprised to learn that the 1899 Wartburgs were already being raced with considerable verve, recording dizzy velocities up to 60 km/h (37 mph). By 1902 Wartburg had the confidence to construct its own 3.1-litre, 15 hp large saloon: the racing version had a five-speed gearbox and could reach 120 km/h (75 mph), enough to gain victory in a Frankfurt international race meeting in August that year.

A new name
Probably the best-known cars to come from the Eisenach works were those sold under the Dixi nameplate. Displayed at the 1904 Frankfurt International Automobile Show, the first Dixi models were designed by Willy Seck and proved that the Eisenach factory was fully established as manufacturers and designers. There was a choice of two models: the S6 and S12. The figures referred to horsepower, the two-cylinder S6 providing 6 hp and the four-cylinder S12 approximately 12 hp. The S12, originally 2815 cc, proved versatile and was the basis of many similar descendants that remained in production, with due interruptions for wartime priorities, until 1925.

PRECEDING PAGES *In 1924 there were 2194 employees at the Eisenach factories, which made Dixi cars and trucks. The latter are seen leaving the picturesque works in that year. Like BMW— who took over in 1928— Eisenach had also made aero engines.*

LEFT *The charm of the perky 1929 DA 1 Dixi 3/15 two-seater is still obvious more than 50 years after the last of these 4831 machines was built. Mechanically they were closely related to the original Austin Seven, including a three-speed non-synchromesh gearbox and a 748 cc engine.*

RIGHT *By 1931 the BMW influence on the basic Austin-Dixi design had become even more obvious. This DA 4 model boasted four-wheel cable brakes worked via the pedal instead of the Dixi's rear-only pedal operation. From 1931 to '32 some 3000 BMW DA 4s were manufactured at Eisenach.*

BMW 3/15 Limousine (1929–32)

ENGINE

No. of cylinders	4 in-line
Bore/stroke mm	56 × 76
Displacement cc	748.5
Valve operation	Side camshaft, short pushrods to side valves
Compression ratio	5.6:1
Induction	Solex sidedraught carburettor
BHP	15 at 3000 rpm

DRIVE TRAIN

Clutch	Single dry plate
Transmission	Non-synchromesh 3-speed gearbox and propshaft drive to rear axle

CHASSIS

Frame	Separate tubular chassis
Weight kg	485 to 535
Wheelbase mm	1900
Track – front mm	1000
Track – rear mm	1030
Suspension – front	Originally transverse sprung axle (DA 2); DA 4 simply transverse spring
Suspension – rear	Live axle with quarter springs
Brakes	Cable operated on 4 wheels
Tyre size	27 × 4". Typ DA 4: 4.00 × 18
Wheels	Wire spoke with disc covers

PERFORMANCE

Maximum speed	75 km/h (47 mph)
Fuel consumption	6 litres/100 km (47 mpg)
Number built	6600 DA 2 Limousines; 2575 DA 4 Limousines. Altogether 15,948 BMW-badged 3/15 hp models made

Before World War 1 there was a variety of Dixi products to choose from, with truck production becoming the mainstay of the business until 1921. That year the company was taken over by Gothaer Waggonfabrik AG, but this famous manufacturer of railway coaches and military aircraft was not in the best of health after the postwar ban on German warplane production, so it was no surprise that the business steadily deteriorated through the 1920s. Part of the Gothaer business belonged to a well-known motor industry speculator, Jacob Schapiro, and he soon acquired majority control over the Eisenach/Dixi concern. As part of his plan to fight the deepening recession in the German market, Schapiro incorporated the Cyklon six-cylinder car range, from another of his factories, with the Dixi models of 1926. Still sales sagged and by 1927 even cycle manufacture was abandoned in favour of an exciting and highly successful small-car project.

A British rescuer

By 1927 a minor miracle was necessary to keep the 1200 employees gainfully at work. However, Schapiro had found just what was needed, even though it was a design rejected for manufacture under licence by other German makers of the period. In Britain it was simply called the Austin Seven and Schapiro's direct negotiations with Sir Herbert Austin brought the British baby two-seater to Germany—and a mass production line to Eisenach at about the same time as Daimler-Benz was also introducing assembly line production.

The first 100 Austins went to Germany in right-hand drive form, similar to the model that had been such a success in Britain since its

sufficiently high production standard to meet military demand (over 200 were required). Still firmly wedded to military aero engines, the embryo BMW company progressed from being that 1917 limited liability concern (GmbH) to one with stockholders and public shares (AG) on 13 August the following year.

At the end of World War 1 in November 1918 the Bavarian aero engine company emerged fit and strong under the managerial and engineering influence of Max Friz. Less than a year after the war ended a Friz-designed six-cylinder engine installed in a DFW biplane established an astonishing altitude record of 9700 m (31,826 ft). This was achieved from an airfield on what is now Munich's Olympiapark and is opposite BMW's modern four-cylinder shaped headquarters building. At the time there were aircraft production facilities there that included part of the present factory area, so local pride was assured when aviation records were set in the immediate postwar period. However, the BMW name had been sold to Knorr Bremse AG: the intention was to turn the concern into a mere production facility concentrating on braking equipment for railway carriages and the like! It was 1922 before one of BMW's original trustees and principal investors, Viennese financier Camillo Castiglioni, managed to buy back again both the BMW name and the assets of Bayerische Flugzeugwerke AG; to pay for these he used German currency that was by then becoming worthless. It was this reborn concern that used the round blue-and-white trademark in advertising designed to sell its engines for many purposes outside aviation, including boating and agriculture.

Friz had designed a flat-twin motorcycle engine of just under 500 cc and this was offered to other motorcycle manufacturers in

LEFT *The Dixi S16 had one of the longest production lives of Eisenach's cars—it was made from 1911 until the mid-1920s. The long-stroke four-cylinder engine was increased in power from 32 to 39 bhp during production of just 710 examples.*

RIGHT *The 3/20 AM series marked BMW's full commitment to designing cars of its own. This 1932 AM 4 is one of 7215 from the 1932–4 AM 1–4 series. All used a 782 cc development of the four-cylinder unit that originally came from Austin.*

announcement in 1922. The 750 cc Sevens had the Dixi radiator mascots attached and were on sale in 1927 as Dixi 3/15 Typ Da 1s. Acceptance of the 75 km/h (47 mph) licensed Austin, with its fuel consumption of 6 litres/100 km (47 mpg), was immediate. Although only some 250 Wartburg-badged cars had been sold between 1899 and 1903, Dixi production amounted to over 15,000 units, of which more than 9000 were licensed versions of the Austin. Yet even this was not enough to prevent a BMW take-over in 1928.

While it is easy to trace the links between Wartburg, Dixi, Cyklon and eventual BMW control, describing some of the dealing that went on before BMW was able to acquire that Eisenach car factory is more complex. The story begins with aero engines and the establishment of the Bayerische Flugzeugwerke AG (Bavarian Aircraft Works) in March 1916. This company was itself the result of a merger between the Karl Rapp Motorenwerke and the Gustav Otto Flugmotorenfabrik, a liaison that had come about in 1913. The name Bayerische Motoren Werke (BMW) was first used in July 1917 and reflected the diversification of the company born of that merger. Engineer Karl Rapp was associated with a number of aero engines of varying success, and was a driving force within the new company as it struggled to produce engines such as the Austro-Daimler V12 to a

Germany, and then installed by BMW itself in a frame marketed as the Helios. Finally BMW was drawn into the bike business with the 1923 R 32 design which used the company's own running gear and frames. This featured two key parts of the present-day BMW motorcycle, the air-cooled flat twin *boxer* engine and the shaft drive to the rear wheel (the engine was called *boxer* because the cylinders 'boxed' each other). The same year brought the resumption of aero engine manufacture, and BMW was also taking part in two-wheel competition by 1924, just a year after motorcycle production was resumed.

By 1925 BMW was becoming so interested in the possibilities of producing its own cars that negotiations were started with the famous aerodynamicist and engineer Wunibald Kamm. Based near Stuttgart, Kamm had produced an advanced two-cylinder *boxer*-engined car with front-wheel drive and all-independent suspension. BMW investigated this 1030 cc vehicle to the extent of having a small number of running prototypes made between 1925 and 1927, but it was apparent that it would not proceed with its own design, a decision ratified by the company board in July 1928.

The entrepreneur Castiglioni was influential in persuading BMW senior management and large shareholders that, while it might run

10

against some of their interests to produce a rival to the Daimler-Benz cars of the period (that former BMW luminary, Schapiro, was the leading D-B shareholder!), a small car would be perfectly feasible. It was through Castiglioni that BMW started to talk seriously to Eisenach's Dixi representatives, even though BMW itself was in debt, thanks to the poor trading conditions in Germany at the time.

The agreement

An increase in shareholding capital from 10 to 16 million Reichsmarks enabled BMW to change the name of the Eisenach Dixi factory to that of Bayerische Motoren Werke for the sum of 10 million RM. It was not a particularly good deal as Eisenach turned out to have 7.8 million RM in hidden debts and these had to be taken on too, but the agreement was ratified by 16 November 1928. From January 1929 onwards the Dixi symbol disappeared from the 3/15 models and Britain's transplanted Austin Seven became the first BMW car: the BMW 3/15 Typ DA 2. The 'DA' part of the designation stood for *Deutsche Ausführung*, or German version.

At first the new owners were simply content to watch output soar, leaving the Seven completely alone. In 1929 over 5300 of the BMW 3/15s were made and nearly 6800 the following year—encouraging figures for a period of intense recession in the motor industry.

Given the dynamic and volatile nature of the entrepreneurs and engineers at BMW it could not be long before they began to express their own ideas in car production. In July 1929 the 3/15 took on a new radiator shape and larger doors, and the open two-seater model was made without the running boards it had previously. These models were referred to as DA 2s and were important for their fitting of four-wheel brakes to replace the rear-only excitement of the DA 1's system.

The DA 2 was made until 1931, with a parallel sports model from 1930 to 1931. Not only did this confirm BMW's continued competitive inclination, on two wheels or four, but it also marked a brief return of the Wartburg name under BMW ownership, as the sports DA 3 model was designated BMW Wartburg. With a low overall height—less than 1016 mm (40 in) with the screen folded—and an extra 3 hp obtained from a raised engine compression ratio (7:1 instead of 5.6:1) the little BMW hybrid was capable of over 80 km/h (50 mph) and better than 7.06 litres/100 km (40 mpg). Some 150 DA 3s were made and, like the original Austin Seven, its toughness was soon proved in a variety of motor sporting events, including first class awards on the 1931 Monte Carlo Rally and racing success amid the grandeur of the 22 km (14-mile) Nürburgring.

On 1 March 1932 BMW struck out on its own, prematurely withdrawing from the agreement to build the Austin Seven, which the company had further developed with an independent front suspension layout (DA 4) that was not very well received. It is not clear whether this was the fault of the talented Friz, as some German sources imply, or because he did not enjoy a good enough working relationship with his design office for them to produce exactly what he had in mind. What is known is that the car was somewhat unpredictable in its steering and handling and that BMW quickly produced a more thoroughly engineered replacement.

Among the BMW directors there were still influential members of the Daimler-Benz board. Liaison between the two companies seemed inevitable. They shared a common wartime interest in aero engine production and a vigorous attitude to competition—although it should be said Mercedes was really at the forefront of Grand Prix and sports car racing, while BMW continued to accrue motorcycle success. Yet when the companies decided to cooperate it was to produce bodies at the D-B Sindelfingen factory for a new BMW, rather than any surprise sporting collaboration.

The Austin contract was cancelled at less than a month's notice, and the launch of the new BMW and its D-B body was planned for 1 April 1932. Because of the continuing recession the new BMW 3/20 AM 1 did not enjoy quite the sales success that the motoring press had forecast, yet it was a very important BMW because it combined the company's engineering and the larger body style to such a degree that it was taken more seriously than the Austin Seven-derived Dixis and BMWs. Most features were new, from the central backbone chassis to the overhead-valve version of the Austin engine which was enlarged from 748.5 to 782 cc by a 2.2 mm increase in stroke. Power was raised from a humble 15 bhp to 20 bhp, enough to provide a comfortable 80 km/h (50 mph). Fuel consumption, however, went from better than 7.06 litres/100 km (40 mpg) to 7.5 litres/100 km (37.6 mpg) because the body weight had increased by some 68 kg (150 lb). The front suspension remained the same as on the criticized DA 4, and its eccentricities were compounded by an independent rear suspension. The 3/20 sold 7215 examples in AM 1, AM 2, AM 3 and AM 4 versions. The biggest change was the adoption of a four-speed gearbox for the AM 2 in the closing months of 1932, but there was no synchromesh offered in any model to the end of production in 1934.

The first BMW six

Considering the role that six-cylinder engines play in current BMW production—every model in the range can have six-cylinder power and it is used in every guise from basic 320 to the advanced turbocharger system employed for the 745i flagship—the company's first six-cylinder car deserves special attention. Shown for the first time at the Berlin exhibition of 1933, the BMW 303 proved that Eisenach was becoming a quality force to be reckoned with in future.

The confidence to become a more sophisticated car manufacturer stemmed from the increasing success of aero engine manufacture, the steadily expanding motorcycle division with its sporting reputation—and car sales figures that placed BMW fifth among German manufacturers. This was achieved at a time when rivals like DKW and Audi had been forced to join forces. Emphasizing that car building was still only part of the business was the fact that out of 4700 staff employed by BMW only 2400 worked on car production.

The emergence of the Nazi party and its policies began to involve BMW increasingly, for aero engines became more and more

LEFT *A 1933 BMW 303 saloon displays the unique 'kidney-style' grille that is retained in much reduced area on today's BMWs. These cars were important for having BMW's first in-line six car engine. Of just 1173 cc, it could manage 90 km/h (56 mph). It was this basic six-cylinder unit that led to many of the subsequent BMW sporting designs, classics that lived on even after World War 2 in many countries besides Germany.*

RIGHT *The breathtaking 315/1 was BMW's first production attempt at making a sports car and it proved both a popular purchase and a competitive racer within its class. Some 240 open two-seaters were delivered, but other bodywork could also be ordered during a two-year production run that ended in 1936. This example is from 1935 and its 1490 cc engine with triple Solex carburettor is still in good health.*

important. A new factory for just that purpose was established at Eisenach in 1935, and started with the development of other military items like infantry and anti-tank weapons in 1936. As part of this expansion the well-known Bramo concern was acquired by the BMW company in 1939.

Despite the inevitable build-up on the military side, BMW's reputation for building quality cars grew throughout the 1930s, and the 303 was the starting point. Designed in Eisenach while Max Friz was absent, the 303 was externally significant for carrying the first of the traditional *Nieren* (kidney) shaped radiator grilles that are retained to this day. Underneath there was a stout tubular steel chassis with 90 mm (3½ in) primary tubing, a much improved independent front suspension and a predictable return to a live sprung rear axle via leaf springs. The steering was very direct, almost like a racing car at two turns lock to lock, and similar in construction to many sports cars in its use of rack-and-pinion principles.

In the 1930s Frazer Nash supplied BMWs to suit British tastes. Typical of this liaison is the 1937 Frazer Nash BMW 319/55. This example has a non-standard exhaust system and other minor departures from production specification. Provided by Mark Garfitt.

The 303's six-cylinder engine, and the base from which increasingly powerful units would be built throughout the 1930s, was essentially the ohv four with the same 56 × 80 mm bore and stroke, with two extra cylinders. The result was a four-bearing (instead of two), six-cylinder engine of 1173 cc that produced 30 bhp. Running on large 16-inch steel disc wheels, the 303 suited the new *Autobahnen* that were being so rapidly constructed. The launch cars had a well-publicized trip around Germany and it was not long before the public recognized the worth of these 90 km/h (56 mph) 303s. Both weight and fuel consumption—the latter recorded at 10.02 litres/100 km (28.2 mpg)—were considerably heavier than before. Yet the reaction seems to have been that the quality of ride,

comfort and handling was worth paying for. Introduced in February 1933, the original saloons were bodied by Daimler-Benz, but later that year bodyshells for production came from Ambi Budd, Berlin. A four-window 303 convertible and a sports two-seater were also made.

Four-cylinder follower

The four-cylinder 309, which came on the market in 1934, brought the same style at a lower price. The 845 cc engine was an enlarged version of the unit previously used in the 3/20, giving 22 bhp and a maximum speed of 80 km/h (50 mph). It was produced in five body styles, all with two doors. BMW sold 2300 of the six-cylinder 303s in 1933–4 and an impressive 6000 of its four-cylinder 309 brother during its 1934–6 production run, but the best seller was to come.

The motorcycle division now offered a variety of flat-twin and single-cylinder bikes. Consequently BMW decided to utilize some of that knowledge in a hybrid car and bike three-wheeler. The idea of delivery vans using bike components dated back to 1929, and a

200 cc version was sold from 1932 and a 400 cc model was produced the following year. They both had a single rear wheel layout with shaft drive and three-speed gearbox. Some 250 of the F 76 in 200 cc trim (which did not require a driving licence to operate) were sold during 1932 and 1933, and 350 of the bigger F 79 in 1933. The little delivery wagons were quite useful, but as the opposition from Tempo and Goliath became more sophisticated BMW lost interest; but the company made some prototype two-seater cars on the same principle: these were built in Munich, not Eisenach.

BMW's designations

Both the 309 and its larger capacity successor, the 315, which was produced between 1934 and 1937, brought a logic to BMW's designations and initiated a system still in use today after an intermission in the 1950s and '60s of often bewildering badgework. For example, the 3 in the 309 designation indicated the type of model, and 09 the size of engine, in this case 0.9 litres. By the 1980s

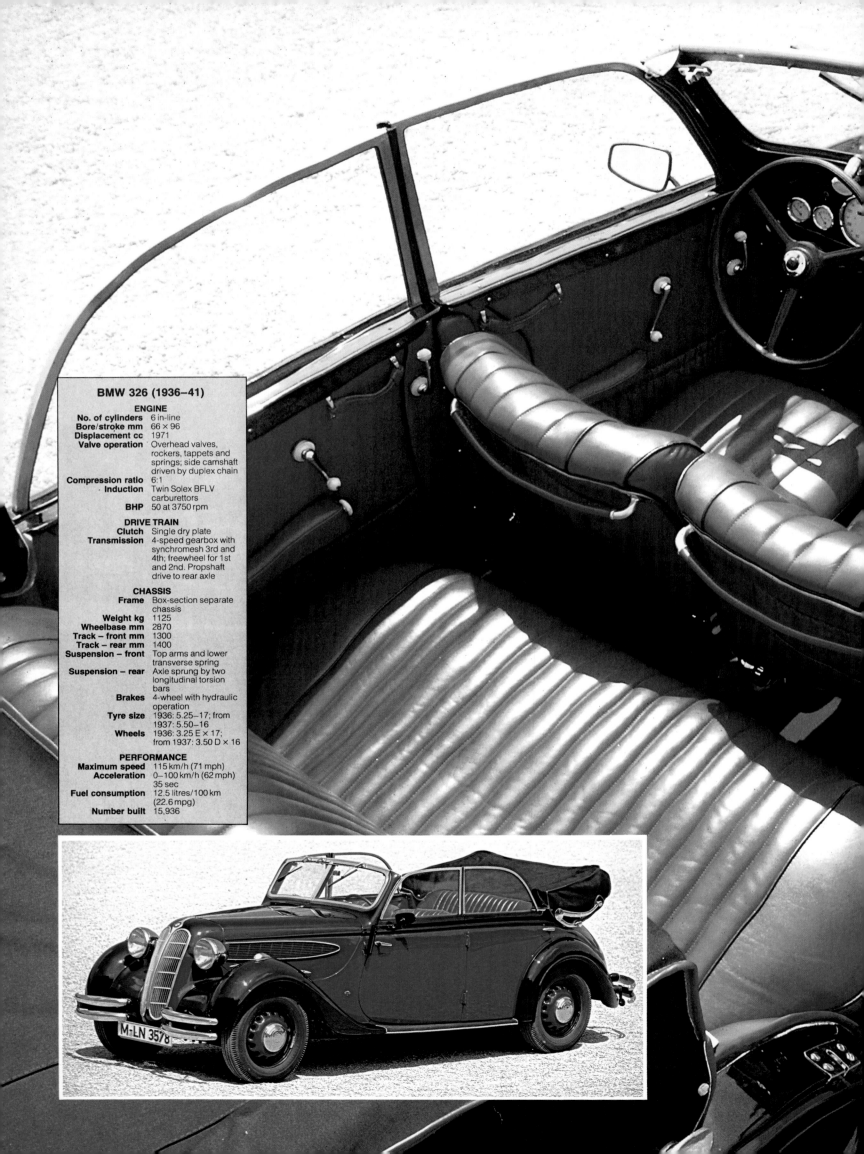

BMW 326 (1936–41)

ENGINE

No. of cylinders	6 in-line
Bore/stroke mm	66 × 96
Displacement cc	1971
Valve operation	Overhead valves, rockers, tappets and springs; side camshaft driven by duplex chain
Compression ratio	6:1
Induction	Twin Solex BFLV carburettors
BHP	50 at 3750 rpm

DRIVE TRAIN

Clutch	Single dry plate
Transmission	4-speed gearbox with synchromesh 3rd and 4th; freewheel for 1st and 2nd. Propshaft drive to rear axle

CHASSIS

Frame	Box-section separate chassis
Weight kg	1125
Wheelbase mm	2870
Track – front mm	1300
Track – rear mm	1400
Suspension – front	Top arms and lower transverse spring
Suspension – rear	Axle sprung by two longitudinal torsion bars
Brakes	4-wheel with hydraulic operation
Tyre size	1936: 5.25–17; from 1937: 5.50–16
Wheels	1936: 3.25 E × 17; from 1937: 3.50 D × 16

PERFORMANCE

Maximum speed	115 km/h (71 mph)
Acceleration	0–100 km/h (62 mph) 35 sec
Fuel consumption	12.5 litres/100 km (22.6 mpg)
Number built	15,936

the complete range followed the same logical system, so that the four current series numbers—3, 5, 6, and 7—precede the capacity in litres, e.g. a 518 is a 5 series 1.8-litre car, and so on.

The 315 of 1934 continued the basic 303 six-cylinder theme and was mechanically very similar, except for the larger bore and longer stroke of the engine, which now provided 34 bhp from its 1490 cc. As the car was little heavier than its predecessor, 315 owners found they obtained much the same fuel consumption as before. However, the 315 was capable of more than 100 km/h (62 mph). As with all models back to the 303, synchromesh was provided on the upper three ratios of the four-speed gearbox.

The foundation of BMW's sporting prowess on four wheels had been laid with some of the Austin Seven derivatives, but strictly speaking, the 315—with 9765 sold the second most popular car in the prewar range—really started the sporting reputation. In the summer of 1934 BMW decided to add to the five body styles already offered on the 315 (the saloon bodywork was by far the most popular choice, as it had been with the 303 and 309). The latest model not only looked good, but also received a power boost.

This two-seater was the BMW 315/1. From its two-tone colour scheme to its flowing tail, the 315/1 had all that was needed to encourage enthusiasts to seek out the 242 examples made from 1935 to 1936. The engine received triple Solex carburettors to replace the normal twin-carb 315 arrangement, and the compression ratio was raised from 5.6 to 6.8:1. The result was another 6 bhp (40 bhp at 4300 rpm) and a BMW guarantee that 120 km/h (75 mph) could be exceeded. You could also travel a little further if you did not use this extra performance all the time, for the fuel tank size was increased to 15 litres (3.3 UK gal) providing a 444 km (276-mile) range at the average 11.5 litres/100 km (24.56 mpg) quoted for the 315/1. Naturally fuel economy was not the burning priority for most customers, who went out and demonstrated that there were few faster 1½ litres in Europe at the time, either in racing or rallying. There were awards on the tough Alpine international rally, outright victories in smaller events, and class racing success at the Nürburgring.

The BMW six-cylinder engine continued to progress under the engineering direction of former Horch employee Fritz Fiedler and a 2-litre 319/1 development also appeared in 1934 and was phased out with the 315/1 in 1936. At first the 1911 cc in-line six of the 319/1 was made with the triple carburettors and raised compression ratio for sporting use in 55 bhp form, when 130 km/h (81 mph) was within reach in ex-factory, unmodified form. This was a useful competition car too, weighing little more than the 315/1, but the point was that the engine proved so adaptable. BMW took the unusual step of reducing power for a series of mechanically similar but visually different BMWs. These were the 1935–7 saloons, convertibles and tourers with 45 bhp twin-carburettor engines that were designated just 319 and 329. These were relatively popular; some 6646 of the 319 were sold, but only 1179 of the 329 (mostly four-window convertibles). However, there was a dramatically better BMW motor car in production by then.

A bigger BMW

The 326 was a tremendously appealing car; its flowing lines made it a major attraction at the 1936 Berlin motor show, and stood the test of time by appearing in a number of designs of the 1950s. It was not a sporty machine: the four-door bodywork was entirely new to BMW and designed to appeal to the potential Mercedes customer as well as BMW's traditional clientele. New features included hydraulics for the four-wheel drum brakes, torsion bar springing for the live rear axle, a new design of independent front suspension and a stout box frame to replace the previous tubular chassis; the rack-and-pinion steering system of the 315 and 319 survived. The engine was basically the same in-line six as before but a slight increase in cylinder bore gave 1971 cc and an unstressed 50 bhp at a peaceful 3750 engine crankshaft rpm.

The 326 was the most popular prewar BMW, selling 15,936 examples; more than 10,000 of these were the four-door saloon with

Magnificent car in an equally fine setting. This BMW 327 cabriolet is from 1938; production ran from 1937 to 1941. A top speed of 126 km/h (78 mph) was possible from the 55 bhp engine. Provided by BMW and owned by Henry Ingster.

BMW 328 (1936–40)

ENGINE

No. of cylinders	6 in-line
Bore/stroke mm	66 × 96
Displacement cc	1971
Valve operation	Overhead V-pattern valves driven by side camshaft, via rockers, tappets and springs
Compression ratio	7.5:1
Induction	Triple downdraught Solex 30 JF carburettors
BHP	80 at 4500 rpm

DRIVE TRAIN

Clutch	Single dry plate
Transmission	Choice of 4-speed gearboxes

CHASSIS

Frame	Separate tubular chassis
Weight kg	830
Wheelbase mm	2400
Track – front mm	1153
Track – rear mm	1220
Suspension – front	Lower arms and transverse top spring
Suspension – rear	Live axle and half elliptic leaf springs
Brakes	4-wheel, hydraulic operation, drums
Tyre size	5.25 or 5.50–16
Wheels	3.25 or 3.50 D × 16 with optional centre knock-off nut

PERFORMANCE

Maximum speed	150 km/h (93 mph)
Fuel consumption	14.5 litres/100 km (19.48 mpg)
Number built	462

its Ambi Budd steel body. Performance of this 1125 kg (2480 lb) saloon amounted to a fine 115 km/h (71 mph) top speed and an average fuel consumption of 12.5 litres/100 km (22.6 mpg).

The 326 was in production from 1936 and survived the early war years, finally being withdrawn in 1941. It was joined in July 1937 by an essentially shorter and lighter two-door cousin called the 320 (which had the old 319 suspension at the front). The first 640 of these had the older 1911 cc six, but this was replaced by the 1971 cc unit. Also related in a typically BMW cross-pollination process was the 321, which was similar to but smaller than the 326, and actually adopted that car's front suspension and rear hinged doors.

The BMW sports car

The next logical step would have been the appearance of sporting versions of the 326, but it was 1937 before BMW presented these outstanding developments (the 327 and 327/28) for the company had decided to introduce a true classic into the range a year before. In June 1936 Ernst Henne, the renowned BMW motorcycle racer, demonstrated the latest and so far most classic BMW design of all: the 328 two-seater sports car. With a combination of the developed 315/319 sports tubular chassis (with box-section crossmembers) and the new Fiedler-inspired aluminium cylinder head for the 1971 cc engine, BMW managed to produce a magical moment in sports car engineering (it made an impact rather like the original Jaguar E-type in the 1960s). It had flowing lines that complemented a well-balanced chassis and had adequate engine power. The suspension was the familiar BMW independent at the front and leaf spring at the rear, with that rack-and-pinion steering of excellent

response, but there was the added braking capability of a hydraulic system. There was a choice of gearboxes from Hurth and ZF, both four-speed (the ZF was more suitable for competition). It was possible to have other competition-inspired features like doubling the fuel tank capacity, or wheels with one centre lock instead of five-bolt fixing, making wheel changes much quicker.

The bulk of 328s were produced in 1937–9, when production ran at over 100 examples a year. Only a couple were made for competition in 1936, the year of the 328's début, and fewer than ten in 1940. Most of the 462 produced had the flowing Eisenach two-seater open body, but specialist coachbuilders like Gläser, Wendler, Drauz and Weinberger also completed 328s. In addition, the factory raced in 1940 two very special closed streamlined coupés and three sleek and open machines. In the Mille Miglia that year they were unsurprising victors against Alfa Romeo opposition. The light closed coupés reached 209 km/h (130 mph), and a closed example shared by Fritz Huschke von Hanstein, later Porsche's competition manager, and Walter Bäumer, set up the winning pace at 166.7 km/h (103.6 mph).

More than 150 examples of the 328 are reckoned to have survived in original form, one of which was still receiving praise from the Editor of *Motor* in a reappraisal of its vigour and handling in the 1980s. It should be remembered that both AFN in London Road, Isleworth (now Porsche dealers), and Bristol Cars did their fair share of marketing BMWs in Britain. AFN sold them before the war under the Frazer Nash name, and in the postwar period Bristol steadily developed the 328 engine from its original production 80 hp and 2 litres to 125 bhp and 2.2 litres. Competition versions exceeded these

LEFT *What a way for four or five people to go open-air motoring! This Frazer Nash BMW 329 is from 1937, the last year in which BMW made these 1911 cc sixes. They were offered by the factory with two choices of cabriolet body, or as chassis ready for coachwork. The BMW 329 was capable of 110 km/h (68 mph); 1179 were manufactured. Provided by Sytner of Nottingham.*

RIGHT *The imposing 4840 mm (190½ in) length of the four-door 335 saloon version attracted a very mixed clientele. It was launched in 1938 and phased out in 1941. By then just over 400 BMW 335s had been made, including only 233 saloons. Powered by a 3485 cc six-cylinder engine, it could reach 145 km/h (90 mph).*

figures, of course, and it was obvious just what a sturdy unit those BMW engineers of the 1930s had provided. Fritz Fiedler spent the early postwar years in Britain, engineering both Bristol and AFN development.

From 1938 to 1940 BMW offered the 80 hp triple Solex carburettor power unit for the 327 in 327/28 form. The car was reckoned to reach 140 km/h (87 mph) compared with the 328's advertised 150 km/h (93 mph) in standard trim. Fuel consumption for both models was estimated at 14.5 litres/100 km (19.48 mpg). Some 569 BMW 327/28s were made, nearly 500 of them sports convertibles.

The final important prewar BMW model was the 335, a four-door extension to the 326 theme, with a single-carburettor engine of 3.5 litres that was of initial interest to the British importers. No firm orders materialized in time to beat the imposition of wartime restrictions on materials, so a little over 400 of these long 4840 mm (190½ in) cars were made in 1938–41. The 335s proved popular with senior military officers and were really large-scale versions of the 326, endowed

with a fuel consumption of 15.96 litres/100 km (17.7 mpg) and a bulk of 1300 kg (2866 lb).

Technically interesting for their four-wheel steering, four-wheel drive and armour plating that brought deadweight to over 1750 kg (3860 lb) were the BMW 325 Jeep-style military vehicles of which 3225 examples were constructed in the 1937–40 period. They did not carry the BMW emblem although they were equipped with the company's 1971 cc six-cylinder engine. The badge was absent because the contract was completed to meet a military specification for which other German car companies also supplied externally similar vehicles with their own power plants.

During the conflict, the 325 proved heavy and fragile. In fact BMW also supplied over 2000 of the 303, 309 and 315 for military use in the 1930s and before that the poor little 3/15 used to be dressed up as a mock tank for army manoeuvres! Few of these light military vehicles survived World War 2, BMW earning its reputation through supply of motorcycles and aero engines.

ROUGH RIDE TO RECOVERY

RIGHT *The 502 was externally distinguishable from its 501 predecessor primarily by the chrome strip along its 'waist'. This example is a 1957 3.2-litre V8. Provided by T.T. Workshops.*

BMW 502 3.2-litre (1955–61)

ENGINE
No. of cylinders	8 in 90° V
Bore/stroke mm	82 × 75
Displacement cc	3168
Valve operation	Overhead valves
Compression ratio	7.2:1
Induction	Single twin-choke downdraught Zenith 32 NDIX carburettor
BHP	120 at 4800 rpm
Torque	209 Nm (154 lbf. ft) at 2500 rpm

DRIVE TRAIN
Clutch	Single dry plate
Transmission	4-speed gearbox

CHASSIS
Frame	Separate chassis
Weight kg	1470
Wheelbase mm	2835
Track – front mm	1330
Track – rear mm	1416
Suspension – front	Double wishbones, longitudinal torsion bars
Suspension – rear	Live axle, torsion bars and 3-point linkage
Brakes	4-wheel hydraulic drums: 1959 options, servo assistance and front disc brakes
Tyre size	6.40 S 15 L
Wheels	4½K × 15

PERFORMANCE
Maximum speed	170 km/h (106 mph)
Acceleration	0–100 km/h (62 mph) 15.0 sec
Fuel consumption	15 litres/100 km (18.83 mpg)
Number built	3935

BELOW *The 501 revived the earlier 1971 cc engine and ensured BMW's presence in the postwar market.*

RIGHT *BMW's 503, based mechanically on the 501/502, was a V8 sports car with 140 bhp and 190 km/h (118 mph). Just over 400 were built.*

For much of the war BMW was a large business with factories not only in Munich (mainly aero engines) and Eisenach, but also in Berlin-Spandau, where there was another plant devoted to aero engines. In all over 42,000 people were employed in 1942. For the makers of military radial engines—powering such effective single-seater fighter aircraft as the original Focke Wulf Fw 190—and the 1943 series production BMW 109-003 jet engine, there were bound to be postwar repercussions. Not surprisingly Allied bombing took its toll, particularly at the Milbertshofen plant in Munich, but the main postwar problem was that Eisenach came in the Russian zone and so BMW's car production plant was lost completely. Then the Americans supervised the confiscation of all useful BMW assets as war reparations: it is said no fewer than 16 nations participated in the BMW spoils of war. In Britain a tangible result was the emergence of BMW 328 technology within the Bristol Cars division of the famous aircraft manufacturer.

It could so easily have been the end of the story, but former employees around the two Munich plants did not give up. There was only one answer in the immediate postwar years and that was to work at anything in the hope of getting both your country and yourself back to some semblance of peacetime prosperity. So it is not surprising that BMW came back into car manufacturing via any sort of metalwork production that could be managed. There was plenty of aluminium left around the Munich plant at Milbertshofen (the other factory was taken over by the Americans as an enormous military depot) and the first evidence that workers had cleared the debris and had started production again came in 1946 with the output of pots and pans, followed by bicycles and some agricultural machinery. Behind the scenes the Deutsche Bank arranged the necessary financing; it was the bank's Dr Hans Karl von Mangoldt-Reiboldt who became BMW's chairman on the board of trustees and occupied this position until 1958. (The operational board chairmanship of BMW has often been a post of long service: BMW's first chairman, military aero engine expert Franz Popp, served from 1928 to 1942.)

Inevitably motorcycles led the postwar revival of BMW on the roads of the West with an appearance at the Geneva show in 1948, followed by some deliveries, of the single-cylinder R 24. Yet it was in East Germany that most initial progress was recorded. Even in 1945 under its new Russian control, the Eisenach works was capable of making 68 BMW-badged 321s, exactly like the prewar design. A state-controlled agency, Autovelo, began marketing these prewar types and they were sold as BMWs until 1949. Then much the same cars, modified with even ghastlier pseudo-American styling, were sold as EMWs—for example, the EMW 327 and 340, which both used the 1971 cc six of the 1930s. Finally the East Germans decided against producing any more of these no longer appealing prewar designs and the last Eisenach EMW 340 was made in 1955, the Wartburg three-cylinder two-stroke unit by now firmly established in the wake of these reborn BMWs.

The Western road back

Meanwhile, in Munich, the car-building dream persisted despite an initial absence of materials and a factory! A number of BMW *aficionados* made what they could of the BMW 328 technology that had not gone to Bristol in England. These included Alexander Freiherr von Falkenhausen, who was behind the AFM (this was a BMW derivative; another example was Veritas), and was a most influential figure in later BMW history: he became the company's power unit engineering director. AFM took its name from Falkenhausen's initials with an 'M' for Munich suffix. The AFM was a sports racing machine, which von Falkenhausen drove with some success. A shortage of vital parts such as bearings led to his return to engineering employment at BMW in 1954. Veritas was a much more ambitious venture run by a group that included former BMW development engineer Ernst Loof. The concern made both sports and racing cars from 1948 to 1953 based on the BMW 328 engine but with its own bodywork. Loof returned to BMW when the Veritas venture failed.

Inside BMW there was immediate confusion as to the type of car the firm wanted to make; a two-seater prototype of 600 cc had been produced but some of the directors felt this did not measure up to

BMW's prewar image and so they decided on a luxury car. It was unfortunate that BMW chose this course as in these years of postwar austerity there was no immediate demand for such a vehicle.

In April 1951 BMW displayed the first prototype of this car: the six-cylinder 501. It had generous flowing lines over its 4724 mm (186 in) length and was powered by a 65 bhp version of the 1971 cc engine that had also led the postwar revival in the East. The steel body sat over a rugged separate chassis of mixed rectangular box sections and tubular construction. Torsion bar suspension, the same principle as used on the front of the Morris Minor, was adopted front and rear. Rather oddly, the steering involved two systems: the column led down to a pinion and semi-circular gear system that transferred steering impulses down to a lower linkage. The all-drum braking was hydraulically activated and needed every inch of swept area, for the 501 weighed more than 1300 kg (2900 lb). Another peculiarity of the original 501 design was the need for a small driveshaft from the engine to the gearbox, as well as a conventional propshaft to the live back axle. This engine-gearbox shaft and consequent rearward position of the box made the steering column gearchange a somewhat cumbersome affair. The primary shaft was dropped on later models.

When that first 501 was shown, BMW really had no means of mass producing it. The company had decided to invest all its available capital in its own pressed steel stamping plant, but that would not be fully operational before the mid-1950s. The temporary answer was to

go to coachwork specialists Baur in Stuttgart and have the bodies made. Even then it was November 1952 before the patient BMW customers began to receive their cars, the styling of which had been completed in Munich, but was variously said to have been inspired by either the prewar 326 or the postwar British Austins. In 1952 only 49 of BMW's first postwar cars reached the public; a more satisfactory 1592 were made in 1953, and 3410 in 1954.

The first V8

From the beginning BMW knew that the 2-litre six-cylinder engine was not really powerful enough to pull such a hefty four-door saloon. In fact the 135 km/h (84 mph) top speed was certainly no disgrace, but the 0–100 km/h (62 mph) acceleration figure of nearly half a minute reflected the considerable task the engine faced. Indeed, the six-cylinder BMW took rather longer to reach a 100 km/h cruising speed than some late 1950s saloons of less than 1 litre.

BMW acted positively to regain its former prestige as suppliers of performance-oriented quality cars: the factory put the long-planned eight-cylinder engine into production. It was Germany's first postwar V8. Of 2580 cc, and made with all its major components in aluminium, BMW's V8 immediately overcame the power problem. Some 95 bhp was provided at the beginning of production in 1954, and 100 bhp by the time this long-lived 2.6-litre entered the 1960s. Few changes were made to the 501 design when the V8 was installed and this was reflected in the designation 502. Externally

BMW 507 (1955–9)

ENGINE
No. of cylinders	8 in 90° V.
Bore/stroke mm	82 × 75
Displacement cc	3168
Valve operation	Overhead valves driven via rockers, tappets and springs from a central camshaft
Compression ratio	7.8:1
Induction	Twin downdraught Zenith 32 NDIX carburettors
BHP	150 at 5000 rpm
Torque	237 Nm (174 lbf. ft) at 4000 rpm

DRIVE TRAIN
Clutch	Single dry plate
Transmission	4-speed gearbox,

CHASSIS
Frame	Shorter wheelbase version of 501/502 box section and tubular separate chassis
Weight kg	1300
Wheelbase mm	2480
Track – front mm	1445
Track – rear mm	1425
Suspension – front	Double wishbones and torsion bars
Suspension – rear	Live axle with leading and trailing arms, Panhard rod and torsion bars
Brakes	Servo-assisted 4-wheel drums
Tyre size	6.00 H 16
Wheels	4.50 E × 16

PERFORMANCE
Maximum speed	190–220 km/h (118–137 mph) according to axle ratio
Acceleration	0–100 km/h (62 mph) 11.5 sec
Fuel consumption	17 litres/100 km (16.6 mpg)
Number built	253

ABOVE *The 700 saloon shown is from the end of the run in 1964. The saloon version became available just after its coupé counterpart; both were announced in 1959.*

RIGHT *The 1961 BMW 250 Isetta was a close-coupled four-wheeler in Germany, but for the British market a three-wheel layout was adopted. With its single-cylinder engine of motorcycle origin, the Isetta had a maximum speed of 85 km/h (53 mph).*

there was a chrome side strip added to the existing lower sill. Mechanically the first gear had a different ratio to suit the V8's extra pulling power. The 502, and from 1955 a V8-equipped 501, performed well taking 10 seconds less to reach 100 km/h and having a top speed of 160 km/h (100 mph). Of course there was a fuel consumption penalty to pay, but this did not seem to worry BMW management as it took only until 1955 for the company to make a bigger version of the V8. Sold as the 502 3.2-litre, and subsequently the basis for much more sporting applications, the later V8 had a longer crankshaft stroke to provide 3168 cc and 120 bhp in its mildest form.

Small car schizophrenia

The large BMWs—and their subsequent sporting derivatives the 503, made from 1956 to 1959, and the glorious 507 of the same period—certainly brought back a measure of the company's previous prestige. However, their low volume sales could not offset the increasing losses being incurred in motorcycle manufacture. By 1953 the German economic boom had propelled BMW to its 100,000th bike of the postwar period. However, motorcycle sales were now declining as the market seemed to want the better weather protection of small and cheap cars.

The Frankfurt show of 1955 neatly demonstrated the BMW dilemma. The company exhibited the Count Albrecht Goertz-

designed 503 and 507 coupé and cabriolet and the Italian-designed Isetta two-seater 'bubble car', for which the Munich company had acquired the manufacturing rights. There could not have been a bigger contrast. The 503 and 507 both echoed the large luxury sports car theme and carried a 3.2-litre V8 punch: the 507 was rated at 150 bhp and was said to be capable of anywhere between 190 and 220 km/h (118 and 137 mph) according to the ratio within the rear axle. Both these sports cars were based on the saloon car running gear, but the 507 had a shorter wheelbase, which contributed much to making it one of the greatest sports car-styling triumphs of the 1950s.

Then there was the Isetta. Styled by ISO and featuring a unique full-width front door as an integral part of its design, it had a four-wheeler layout, the back pair resting on a very narrow track (a single rear wheel was fitted for Britain to take advantage of motorcycle driving licence laws) and its original two-stroke engine was replaced

West Germany of the 1950s there were few takers for a car that combined a daunting initial cost with a 17 litres/100 km (16.6 mpg) fuel consumption, despite the fact that the customer was offered the then useful 0–100 km/h acceleration figure of 11½ seconds.

In autumn 1958 the much talked-of amalgamation or demise of BMW because of financial losses looked all too real. BMW had lost 12 million DM that year, paying off 6.5 million by exhausting the capital reserves and leaving a 5.5-million DM loss to be carried into 1959. That year there was a 9.2-million DM adverse balance and nearly half the shareholders' capital had to be depleted in preserving the company's existence. Throughout 1959 the management threshed ineffectively against its increasing liabilities, seeking further bank credits and even support from the Bavarian state.

It was against this background, and a drop in motorcycle sales from nearly 30,000 a year in 1954 to little over 5400 in 1957, that BMW was struggling to fill the gap in its car model range. At the top end there were the fast and rapidly ageing big V8 saloons and sports cars. Then there was a huge model gap until the 600 and the Isettas. The 600, however, was not just another loss maker that was neither car nor bubble car proper, for the independent rear suspension was of the semi-trailing type that has since become standard on all BMWs, and many other prestige models from manufacturers such as Mercedes-Benz, Rolls-Royce, Opel and Ford. The advantage of the BMW system at the time—and it has since been modified to keep pace with modern tyres and roadholding demands—was simply the combination of a comfortable ride with good cornering capability.

BMW began its attempt to bridge that gap with the 700. Mechanically it amounted to much the same recipe as the 600, with trailing arms and rear motorcycle-type engine, but it was clothed in a rakish two-door coupé body by Michelotti of Turin. Ready for sale by August 1959, the coupé rather unusually preceded the saloon version, also of 30 bhp and 697 cc, which was put on the market in December the same year. Both went on to become great successes in the 1960s and were also produced in a later long-wheelbase version until September 1965, when 188,121 had been constructed, around 150,000 of them in the 120 km/h (75 mph) saloon guise. The coupé was reckoned to be slightly faster, but they were both attractive propositions, combining good road manners with perky performance and 7.06 litres/100 km (40 mpg) economy.

A Mercedes division?

As things went from bad to worse in 1958, BMW had already lost the chairman who had done so much to get the company back into the motor business in the immediate postwar years. Kurt Donath retired towards the end of 1957. Dr Heinrich Richter-Brohm took over, steering BMW towards that elusive goal: a middle-class car of around 1½ litres to sell to the more discerning middle-class buyer, the category that was fast emerging as a most important economic force among West German consumers.

While the new car could be planned by a team that included Alex von Falkenhausen at the head of the engine design department, putting it into production against a background of ever-worsening BMW financial results looked impossible. Indeed the annual general meeting held on 9 December 1959 was a dramatic occasion, for the chairman of the board of trustees, Dr Hans Feith, demonstrated just how the Deutsche Bank saw the future. He proposed a redevelopment plan that really amounted to a relatively low-priced Mercedes take-over bid. The bank was also a large shareholder in the Mercedes-Benz company. Further meetings showed that the board had little to offer as an alternative to the Mercedes acquisition, except bankruptcy, although there were said to be plenty of other companies outside Germany interested in buying BMW, particularly in Britain and America.

Nevertheless the smaller BMW shareholders and the dealerships across Germany stuck out for an independent BMW. Grouped together against the Mercedes, or any other take-over plan, the opposition appointed the Frankfurt lawyer and accountant Dr Friedrich Mathern. He succeeded in revealing some anomalies in the way the 700 had been financed and this, together with other points raised regarding the future ownership of the company, provided the BMW action group with a lot of muscle. Shortly afterwards Dr Richter-Brohm resigned from the chairmanship of BMW.

Now all that was needed was some money to make that new middle-class car that was to save BMW.

by a BMW R 25 single-cylinder motorcycle unit. Originally 247 cc, the Isetta was later augmented by a 297 cc engine of 1 hp more (13 bhp in all). BMW made 161,728 Isettas between 1955 and 1962. They were capable of just over 80 km/h (50 mph) and 5.5 litres/100 km (51.36 mpg), and provided the basis for a proper four-wheeler car. Complete with trailing-arm independent rear suspension, one side door and the '600' version of BMW's legendary *boxer* twin-cylinder motorcycle engine, the BMW 600 with its bubble car styling laid the foundations for the series of rear-engined BMW 700 saloons and coupés produced from 1959 to 1965. These were proper small cars, which did much to help BMW through the difficult transition from the 1950s to 1960s.

Increasing losses

The 103 km/h (64 mph) BMW 600 was produced from 1957 to 1959: although more than 35,000 were made, the design was not a financial success and BMW losses kept increasing. This was particularly understandable on the car side, as the six- and eight-cylinder saloons had small sales success. In 1958 BMW made about 150 of the 501, which was discontinued from series production thereafter, having reached a total volume of nearly 9000 units in 501 and in later 501/6 trim. The 2.6-litre 502 and 501 V8 sold extremely slowly after 1959, eventually reaching around 9000 sales after ten years, and the final version (the 2600L) was dropped in 1964.

The bigger V8 models really were exclusive. The 3.2 saloons reached a sales zenith of 564 in 1958 and were also to retire in the 1960s after less than half as many examples as had been sold of the smaller eight. The 503 sports car may have been able to dash from 0 to 100 km/h (62 mph) in 13 seconds and reach nearly 194 km/h (120 mph) but only 50 customers bought one in 1959, and only 412 were made in five years of extremely limited production. The 507 was much the same, with only 48 customers in 1959 and 253 sold in total, of which fewer than 100 have survived. Even in the fast-prospering

THE SENSATIONAL SIXTIES

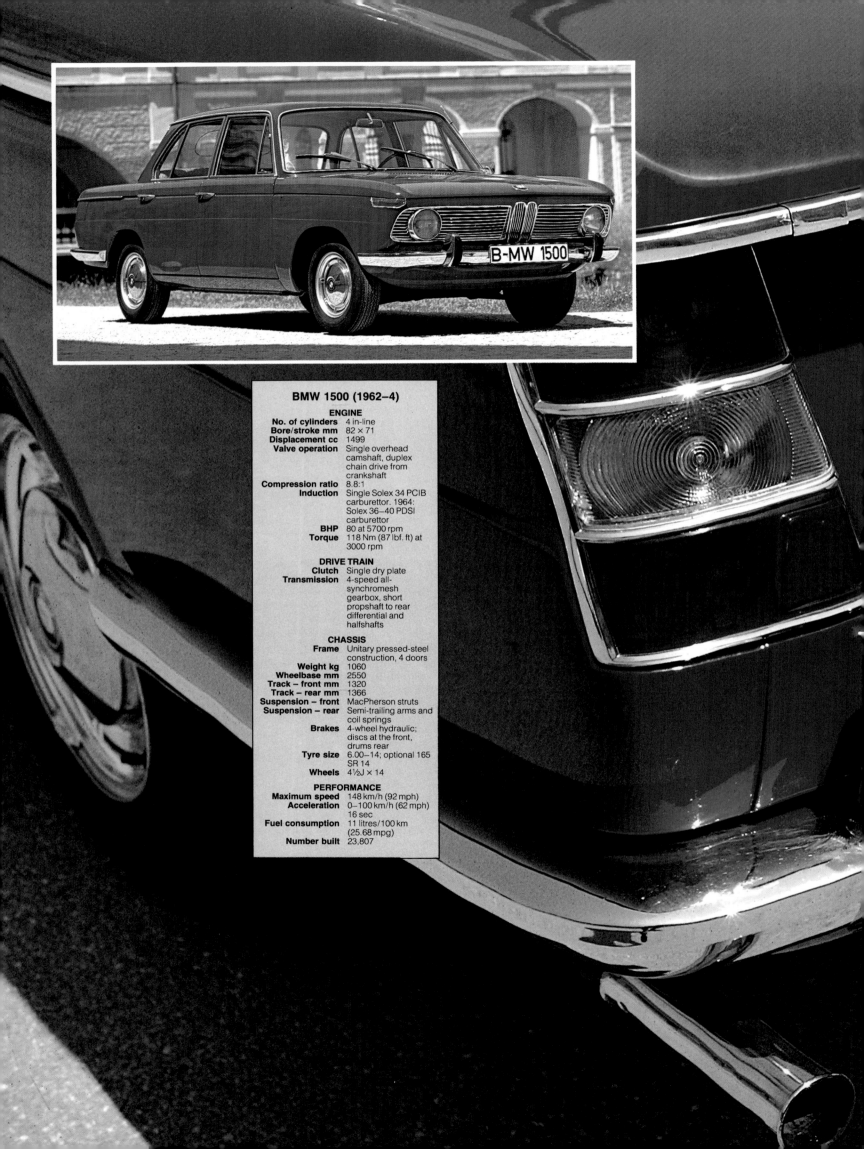

BMW 1500 (1962–4)

ENGINE

No. of cylinders	4 in-line
Bore/stroke mm	82 × 71
Displacement cc	1499
Valve operation	Single overhead camshaft, duplex chain drive from crankshaft
Compression ratio	8.8:1
Induction	Single Solex 34 PCIB carburettor. 1964: Solex 36–40 PDSI carburettor
BHP	80 at 5700 rpm
Torque	118 Nm (87 lbf. ft) at 3000 rpm

DRIVE TRAIN

Clutch	Single dry plate
Transmission	4-speed all-synchromesh gearbox, short propshaft to rear differential and halfshafts

CHASSIS

Frame	Unitary pressed-steel construction, 4 doors
Weight kg	1060
Wheelbase mm	2550
Track – front mm	1320
Track – rear mm	1366
Suspension – front	MacPherson struts
Suspension – rear	Semi-trailing arms and coil springs
Brakes	4-wheel hydraulic; discs at the front, drums rear
Tyre size	6.00–14; optional 165 SR 14
Wheels	4½J × 14

PERFORMANCE

Maximum speed	148 km/h (92 mph)
Acceleration	0–100 km/h (62 mph) 16 sec
Fuel consumption	11 litres/100 km (25.68 mpg)
Number built	23,807

During the early 1960s BMW's prospects were uncertain. The meetings between the creditors and the company ensured that a start was made with resettling debts. But how quickly the deficits could be made good and what kind of future BMW really had as a top car manufacturer demanded much more attention. In the event, BMW recovered quickly, simply through the sales success of new models; but getting them into production was a saga in itself.

In addition to the personalities already mentioned, Herbert and Harald Quandt, the German financiers, became increasingly important in the early 1960s. They acquired stock—the kind of shareholding that saw them so well represented at Mercedes-Benz—but Herbert Quandt's involvement went much further. This hard-headed businessman became convinced, like many of the BMW staff, that the company's future lay in manufacturing a car for the increasingly important West German middle class. The company was no longer to be divided into supporters of the luxury V8s and the economy 'bubble cars', like the Isetta. What was needed, and had been proposed as far back as 1957, was a car that appealed to this emergent group, so significant for West Germany's postwar revival.

Herbert Quandt took a personal interest in making this a reality. The BMW 700 series, especially the sporting coupés that had been so successful in competition, helped to pave the way, as did the company's formidable prewar and wartime engineering reputation. But what sort of car could fill the gap? BMW called it the *Neue Klasse* and briefed the engineers to provide a vehicle of family size with a 1.5-litre engine, independent suspension front and rear (uncommon at this period), plus straight-line performance and handling that would enhance the BMW reputation for cars with something a little out of the ordinary.

Just to produce a car for the Frankfurt Show of autumn 1961 was problem enough. However, the company engineers realized the car's importance and allowed themselves to be pushed through the development period of the 1500 at an abnormally fast pace. This haste was reflected at Frankfurt, for the 1500 was clearly not ready for production—yet BMW felt the car had to be shown in order to interest potential customers. Another clear indication that the BMW sales department, now headed by former Auto Union marketing director Paul Hahneman, was prevailing over the development engineers was the look of the new 1500. During the count-down period to that public début, the Italian stylists Michelotti were asked to incorporate the traditional BMW kidney grille within the front sheet metal.

However, the power unit was one area where all the development 'bugs' appear to have been eliminated with a thoroughness that was unfortunately not matched in the 1500 chassis and bodywork. The five-bearing four-cylinder engine, complete with chain-driven overhead camshaft, was designed by a six-man team working on a minimal budget under the direction of Alexander von Falkenhausen. The former BMW engines engineering chief stated: 'Then many cars had pushrods and three-bearing crankshafts, but I knew we must have something more.' That something extra lay in an immensely strong basic structure, particularly the iron cylinder block. This has been the basis for successful road and competition engines ever since: the 1499 cc engine with its 82 × 71 mm bore and stroke was the forerunner of the BMW 1.6-, 1.8- and 2-litre units which were still in production 20 years later. The four-cylinder engine also provided the basis for the later six-cylinder units still with us today. In addition, that extremely tough 1500 cylinder block is the foundation both for Europe's most successful Formula 2 racing engine, producing about 310 bhp, and for the turbocharged Grand Prix unit of the 1980s—also 1499 cc, although of very different internal bore and stroke dimensions. Of course, von Falkenhausen's team deliberately made that first 1500 unit strong, but even they would be amazed that it could withstand a minimum of 570 bhp instead of the original 75.

PRECEDING PAGES *The 2002 was the most successful of the 02 designs. This beautiful concours winner is a 1972 example of a car that sold nearly 400,000 units. The 2002 had a top speed of 172 km/h (107 mph). Provided by Derek Waller.*

LEFT *The 1500 was a striking and cleanly executed design offering four-door comfort and a measure of sporty character with reasonable fuel economy, features that have remained with the products of BMW ever since.*

This BMW 3200 CS is from 1965, which was the last year of production. Only 603 of these elegant 200 km/h (124 mph) V8 coupés were manufactured. Their lines, the work of the Italian design team Bertone, largely forecast those of subsequent big BMW coupés, particularly in the cockpit area.

Meanwhile, the 1500 of 1961 had attracted thousands of Deutschemarks in deposits from customers who had ordered the car either at the show, or in the wake of the attendant publicity. The principles of the 1500, and thus those of every succeeding mass production BMW to this day, were established. Among the minor surprises was the use of MacPherson strut front suspension, a type made popular through its use by Ford. The semi-trailing arm rear suspension of the 1500 proved so effective that it has become a feature of luxurious family cars today. The steering system, based on recirculating ball principles and a 17.6:1 ratio, remained in use for the generation of cars after *Neue Klasse* and was only removed with the advent of the 1975 BMW 3-series. Other features on the 1500 that were to find wide public acceptance on an equal variety of models were the roomy four-door bodywork and an efficient braking system built around 10.6 in diameter front discs and 9.8 in diameter rear drums.

That BMW had problems getting the 1500 into genuine mass production is shown by the fact that, although a preliminary series was made in February 1962, full production did not begin until October that year! Some sources report that there were 20,000 orders for the new 1500 by the end of 1961, so BMW's embarrassment during 1962 can well be imagined as fewer than 2000 of the new 1500s were made in that first production year. Even by the end of production, when it was succeeded by the much better quality 1600 of similar design and appearance, BMW had manufactured 'only' 23,807 of the 1500 model.

Early difficulties with the 1500 involved customers too. The rear suspension arms gave problems at their attachment points to the steel body, and owners reported both axle and gearbox transmission troubles. These were the legacy of that hurried and financially cramped development, and were attended to in production. It is worth noting that the engine team increased the compression of the 1500 engine before it went into production, so the official power output was 80 bhp rather than the 75 planned.

Descendants

BMW spent much of the early 1960s dispensing with models that proved less and less profitable following the sales success of the 1500 and subsequent variants. The Isettas were dropped in 1962. The large 501 and 502 V8 saloons ceased production the following year, although similar large cars (the 2600 L, 3200 L and 3200 S) limped on a little longer. The 2600 L, basically a 501/502 shape with minor styling and mechanical refinements, proved the most durable and stayed in production until 1964.

However, large V8-engined cars were not entirely forgotten at BMW in the 1960s. Introduced in 1962, the 3200 CS coupé succeeded the 503 sports cars and indicated the direction BMW was taking with coupés. Only 603 were made before production stopped in 1965. Combining a 200 km/h (124 mph) top speed with harmonious styling—the Italian Bertone design team then included Giorgio Giugiaro, who has earned such a fine reputation for his work on projects as diverse as the VW Golf and Lotus Esprit—the 3200 CS was significant for more than merely being the last V8 BMW has produced to date.

Even the gallant little 700 series, extended in length with the LS saloons of March 1962, and augmented by sporty coupé versions, failed to remain in manufacture beyond 1965. Such was the success of the 1500 that BMW speedily pressed on with plans for bigger engines and coupé derivatives. The first of these 1500 descendants followed a pattern that BMW has since employed with increasing sales success: a 'family' approach to design, in that all BMWs within a series share a similar external appearance with a large number of common mechanical components beneath that skin.

Therefore, in September 1963, the company introduced an 1800 model which was simply a 1773 cc version of the 1500 with an additional chrome strip so that status seekers, or the merely curious, could tell the difference between the two models. Already the 1500 had enhanced the company's reputation as well as putting new vigour into its marketing, and a lot more money into the once depleted bank reserves.

The speed of the recovery at BMW can be gauged from the board's recommendation of a modest 6 per cent dividend for shareholders in 1963. It was the first time the company had been able to pay a dividend of any kind for 20 years. In 1964 the dividend was up to 10 per cent and production of the 1500 and kindred *Neue*

Klasse cars approached 40,000 a year. BMW was still among the smallest of German car manufacturers—only Porsche production was less—but the company, including the motorcycle division in West Berlin, was firmly headed in the right direction.

By 1965 BMW could make some satisfying comparisons with the crisis year of 1959: turnover was five times as great; the labour force had doubled to approximately 12,000; and production was 58,524 vehicles, far above the company's previous records and especially gratifying because of the continuing growth in car sales. BMW has continued this success ever since. Even the fuel crisis of the early 1970s merely levelled out car sales rather than sending them plummeting as in so many sections of the car industry. However, it would be wrong to think that all BMW activities were equally successful. The motorcycles suffered increasing competition from the Far East and have required constant revision—with engines considerably more powerful than those of basically similar design that powered BMW 600 cars in the 1950s. As with the cars, BMW salesmanship has matched the product; emphasizing sporting quality, the company has earned a distinctive place for its motorcycles as an alternative to cheaper and ostensibly faster products from the mass manufacturers.

Family growth

For the 1800, bore and stroke were increased to 84 × 80 mm to provide 90 instead of 80 bhp. Thus the normal 1800 (which was later fitted with a smoother but no more powerful engine) was capable of 162 km/h (100 mph) instead of the original 1500's 148 km/h (92 mph). Since the 1500 had already attracted the attention of small engineering companies that derive a living from improving the performance of mass produced cars, it was no surprise that Munich anticipated any such moves. BMW announced its own 1800 TI, a faster version of the 1800. The 110 bhp TI was put on sale from March 1964, providing 177 km/h (109 mph) *Autobahn* motoring. The twin Solex carburettor version of the engine had its compression increased from 8.6:1 to 9.5:1, but there were few external changes apart from bigger 5 in wide wheels (instead of 4½ in).

The 1800 TI had broad sales appeal but only 200 had to be produced of its competition cousin the 1800 TI/SA to meet sporting regulations. 'TI' simply meant *Touring Internationale*, then the equivalent of the much-abused GT badges that many manufacturers later felt they must have on sporty versions of their saloon cars. 'SA'

stood for *Sonderausführung*, indicating a sporting special. Nearly every aspect of the specification was indeed special, a sure sign that BMW was back on the road to prosperity! Unique features of 1800 TI/SA are detailed in the following chapter on competition. Suffice it to say that a maximum speed of 186 km/h (116 mph) was allied to spirited acceleration unmatched by many 2-litre cars today.

The 1800 TI stayed in production until 1966, but by then both it and the 1800 were overshadowed by the development of a 2-litre engine for much the same square-rigged four-door body. The 2-litre engine first appeared in coupé coachwork, for BMW took the distinctively large window area, with no centre pillar, first seen on the 3200 CS, and grafted it on to lower bodywork mainly derived from the 1500/1800 saloons. In June 1965, some seven months before the introduction of a 2000 saloon, BMW announced the 2-litre coupés. Constructed by Karmann at Osnabrück, the BMW 2000 C and 2000 CS (Coupé and Coupé Sport) kept the wheelbase and track of the saloon models but were slightly longer overall, almost 51 mm (2 in) narrower and over 102 mm (4 in) lower. When the 2-litre saloon models were announced in 1966 it became apparent that the sporting coupés were a little heavier than their four-door brethren.

The 2000 C and CS looked the same, but under the bonnet the former had a single carburettor engine of 100 bhp rather than the twin Solex carburettors, raised compression ratio, and 120 bhp of the CS. Their appearance when introduced seemed controversial as well as original with their wrap-around headlamp enclosure and faired-in rear lights. But this was to be a most successful body in its later form with revised headlamps. Coupés are fashionable products, making it all the more remarkable that from the announcement in 1965 the basic shape would survive a decade and a complete engine transplant, and is still echoed in the current range of coupés.

The four-cylinder coupés were purchased primarily for their looks and comfortable sporting appeal; automatic transmission was made

A British BMW Club member owns this rare 1969 2000 CS— one of about 140 right-hand-drive conversions with UK-style quadruple headlamps. The CS proved much more successful commercially than the 2000 C. Provided by John Giles.

available on the 2000 C and this was a particularly popular option. The automatic gearbox, a ZF three-speed unit, was first offered on a *Neue Klasse* car when it was announced as an option for the 1966 1800. BMW estimated that this knocked about 6 km/h (3.7 mph) off maximum speed and increased fuel consumption to 13 litres/100 km (21.73 mpg), compared to the 12 litres/100 km (23.54 mpg) of the manual 1800. The fastest coupé, the 2000 CS, had a top speed of 186 km/h (115 mph) and could accelerate from 0-100 km/h (62 mph) in 12 seconds. Fuel consumption normally averaged about 13.8 litres/100 km (slightly under 21 mpg).

Between 1965 and 1969 just 2837 of the 2000 C, and 8883 examples of 2000 CS, were made, a healthy trade but nothing compared with the astonishing 43,431 of the BMW 2000 saloon in its first full production year, in 1966. The 2000 used the same 89 × 80 mm 1990 cc engine that the 2000 C had pioneered in 1965, right down to the 100 bhp rating. Also introduced in January 1966 was the 2000 TI saloon which had the twin-carburettor, 120 bhp unit that was also used in the 2000 CS. Performance and fuel consumption were obviously similar to the coupés; the coupé shape gave a marginal top-speed advantage of 6.5 km/h (4 mph). However, the 2000 with its improved carrying capacity and the delightful all-round response of the 2-litre engine seemed to be everyone's period favourite. The 2000 single-carburettor saloon, with a number of cosmetic changes to front and rear lamps, remained in production until 1972. The TI developed a more luxurious character and was designated the 2000 tilux (the process of changing BMW designations from capital letters to lower case, as here, was begun in 1968) and lasted until 1970. Both models were a little

overshadowed by the first fuel-injected BMW road car. This was the 2000 tii of 1969–72, which had the Kugelfischer mechanical system, of racing fame, tamed to provide 130 bhp. These cars were refined in performance and quite fast at 185 km/h (115 mph), but the 1500 to 2000 series had begun to show its age and weight by then. These cars were losing their appeal to a 1966 series that forms the next part of the story. Altogether more than 350,000 *Neue Klasse* BMWs were made, some at the BMW-owned assembly plant in South Africa.

Two-door versatility

The products that probably gave BMW its present fine reputation were the 02 series: the 1602, 1802, 2002 and the 1970s fuel-economy special, the 1502. When the new series was first introduced at the Geneva Motor Show of March 1966, the vehicle was simply known as the 1600-2 to indicate the number of doors the body carried compared to the earlier four-door series. The basic idea was to use the 1573 cc engine, the successor to the original 1500 installed in the BMW 1600 of 1964–6, in a much lighter body. The two-door 1600–2 weighed only 940 kg (2072 lb), compared with 1070 kg (2360 lb) for the equivalent four-door. This meant the 1600-2 could perform better at reduced fuel consumption. BMW reported a half-second improvement in the 0–100 km/h figures, an increase of 8 km/h (5 mph) in top speed, and 11.5 litres/100 km (24.57 mpg), which was nearly as good as the original 1500 and marginally better than the 1600.

These improvements were also coupled with a lower price; this welcome reduction was particularly important in BMW's expanding exports to Britain and the United States. In 1975 the 1600-2 became

LEFT *The 2-litre 2000 was a logical progression from the 1500 and achieved sales of around 150,000. This British concours-winning example shares the 100 bhp 2002 four-cylinder engine, which gives it up to 169 km/h (105 mph). Provided by G.W. Jennings.*

RIGHT *Hatchback prophet! BMW was not the first marque to provide such useful bodywork, but the 1802 Touring certainly typifies the attractive way the company added yet another facet to the versatile 02 series. The 1800 engine provided over 160 km/h (100 mph), almost 11.8 litres/100 km (24 mpg) overall, and acceleration from rest to 100 km/h (62 mph) in under 12 seconds. The Touring was also produced with 1600 and 2000 cc engines.*

the 1602 to accord with the designation of its stablemates, particularly the 2002 of 1968 which combined a two-door body with a 2-litre engine. Until the 2002 arrived, the twin-carburettor version of the 1600, introduced in September 1967 and known simply as 1600 TI, and manufactured for one year only, was intended as the sporty two-door model. The 1600 TI had a 175 km/h (109 mph) performance, but the allure of low down acceleration and inserting the 1990 cc engine in either single-carburettor 100 bhp trim (2002) or twin-carburettor 120 bhp form (2002 TI) proved irresistible, particularly outside Germany. The 2002s were accepted very warmly in Britain and America, where importation and distribution were still in independent hands rather than the factory subsidiaries of today. The 2002 is often said to have been the brainchild of the American importers but, given the way in which BMW has consistently mixed engines for each of its models, it seems unlikely that the factory would not have explored this avenue itself.

From its introduction in 1966 to the end of the economy-conscious 1502 in 1977 (this was made alongside the later 3-series for two years), the 02 derivatives seemed endless. Anticipating future styling, there was even a version with a hatchback third door: the Touring model of the 1970s; the 02 was also available, in limited quantities, as a convertible by Baur in Stuttgart. The success of the 02 cars and the rapid expansion of BMW's car manufacturing capabilities can be judged from the fact that the four-door series of 1962–72 (to 1974 in South Africa) had a total production figure of 364,378. By comparison 863,203 of the 02 machines were made in 11 years. By far the most popular were the 2002 types: nearly 400,000 of these were made between 1968 and 1976.

This sales success is not surprising, for the 2-litre engine provided a balance of speed, some 173 km/h (107 mph), and overall pulling power that was made even more acceptable by good road manners and a fuel consumption of 12.5 litres/100 km (22.6 mpg). Customers kept calling for more power, even though a twin-carburettor 2002 ti, with a 185 km/h (115 mph) maximum speed, was offered from 1968 onwards. Such demands were satisfied in the 1970s, but even during the first years of its life the 02 series could be obtained with power outputs of 85 bhp (1600-2); 105 bhp (1600 TI); 100 bhp (2002); and 120 bhp (2002 ti). The same basic principles found in all the 02 series—but with impressive braking and suspension improvements where appropriate—eventually coped with power outputs ranging from 75 to 170 bhp, and maximum speeds from 157 km/h (97 mph) to 211 km/h (131 mph). Simply to state that the 02 cars were versatile does not adequately convey their merits: these 02 BMWs were truly outstanding cars that satisfied widely differing public taste and demand.

The Glas merger

That BMW was able to manufacture such large numbers of cars, and subsequently expand its range to encompass four primary models, owed a great deal to Hans Glas GmbH. This family car business was at Dingolfing, some 97 km (60 miles) northeast of Munich, and came complete with a wooden factory building, plus a reputation built mainly on production of the Goggomobil, an unfashionable small car. Glas had failed to make the transition from economy cars to the production of a handsome 1700 GT fastback and the glamorous 'Glaserati', a V8 machine that looked like a Italian Frua style that looked like a Maserati to the German public. By 1966 Glas was in the kind of financial trouble that BMW had faced seven years earlier, but for Glas there would be no reprieve. BMW took over its factory site and assets (mainly debts) in 1966, and the following year was partly devoted to marketing BMW-badged Glas cars. BMW planned a future for the Dingolfing site, which has since provided all BMW car output, although most 3-series are still made in Munich.

The Glas cars produced under BMW ownership have an obvious appeal for collectors, as the revised 1700 GT (known as the 1600 GT with appropriate BMW engine and rear suspension) was only manufactured from September 1967 to August 1968. Just 1255 of

A true convertible, but a rare beast both in terms of volume and the unusual 'halfback' roof-cum-rollover bar arrangement. This 1973 2002 Cabriolet is from a very limited production run undertaken by one of BMW's traditional allies in coachbuilding—the firm of Baur at Stuttgart. The Cabriolet represents another interesting variation on the excellent 02 theme. Provided by Peter Rust.

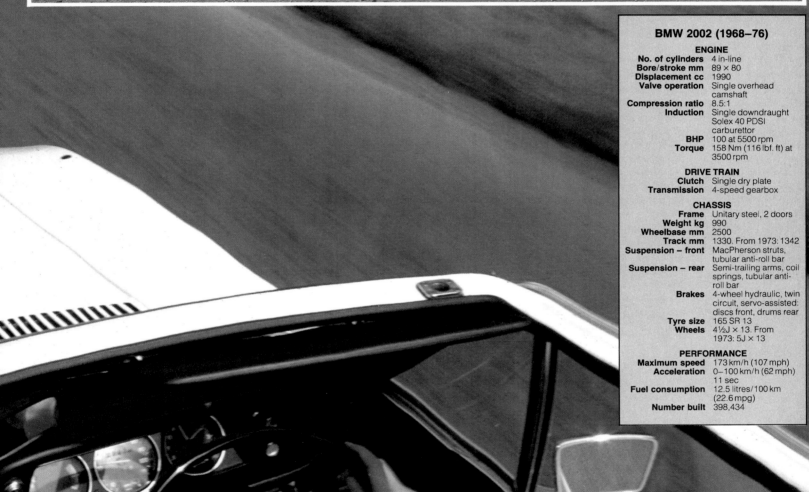

BMW 2002 (1968–76)

ENGINE

No. of cylinders	4 in-line
Bore/stroke mm	89 × 80
Displacement cc	1990
Valve operation	Single overhead camshaft
Compression ratio	8.5:1
Induction	Single downdraught Solex 40 PDSI carburettor
BHP	100 at 5500 rpm
Torque	158 Nm (116 lbf. ft) at 3500 rpm

DRIVE TRAIN

Clutch	Single dry plate
Transmission	4-speed gearbox

CHASSIS

Frame	Unitary steel, 2 doors
Weight kg	990
Wheelbase mm	2500
Track mm	1330. From 1973: 1342
Suspension – front	MacPherson struts, tubular anti-roll bar
Suspension – rear	Semi-trailing arms, coil springs, tubular anti-roll bar
Brakes	4-wheel hydraulic, twin circuit, servo-assisted: discs front, drums rear
Tyre size	165 SR 13
Wheels	4½J × 13. From 1973: 5J × 13

PERFORMANCE

Maximum speed	173 km/h (107 mph)
Acceleration	0–100 km/h (62 mph) 11 sec
Fuel consumption	12.5 litres/100 km (22.6 mpg)
Number built	398,434

these 185 km/h (115 mph) BMW 1600 GTs were made. Rarer still were 389 BMW Glas 3000 V8 models, produced from September 1967 to May 1968. Developed from the 2.6-litre Glas V8, of which 277 examples were produced before the take-over, the 3-litre model was ahead of its time, with belt drive for its overhead camshafts and transistorized ignition. Equipped with a 160 bhp V8, the BMW Glas hybrid could reach 195 km/h (121 mph) and 100 km/h from a standing start in an exciting 10 seconds. However, fuel consumption of the twin- or triple-carburettor engine was a worrying 16 litres/ 100 km (17.65 mpg).

In September 1968 the reason for the disappearance of the Glas marque became apparent. An entirely new coupé was to fulfil BMW's sporting requirements, sharing new running gear with a range of saloon cars marking the company's return to mass produced six-cylinders. Having begun to move motorcycle production from Munich to West Berlin in 1967, and having acquired Glas, BMW was ready for this expansion in its car line; the more so since in 1968 the company had succeeded for the first time in producing more than 100,000 cars a year.

During half a century of endeavour, Bayerische Motoren Werke

had travelled an often tortuous route from military specialists to a settled niche as manufacturers of quality cars for a prospering public. There were nagging fears, however: would the return to six cylinders lead BMW back to the old luxury car days of limited production and falling profits? Had this vigorous Bavarian enterprise, less than a decade after threatened bankruptcy and anticipated capitulation to Mercedes-Benz, permanently recovered? Such questions certainly occupied the minds of both BMW management and of rival companies. The latter had to worry not only about BMW's increasing commercial advance, including a very effective export drive, but also about the less tangible, but nevertheless significant prestige that the company was gaining from its participation in motoring sport.

Advanced—but doomed. The Glas 3000 (in foreground) and the 1700 convertible demonstrated for BMW a number of sophisticated engineering features put into limited production. After taking over the company, BMW did most with the 2982 cc Glas 3000 V8, which featured transistorized ignition in 1967, and had a maximum speed of 195 km/h (121 mph). The 1700, however, was swiftly dropped.

THE
SPORTING
INSTINCT

LEFT On display at the Auto & Technik Museum, Sinsheim, is this magnificent BMW 269 Formula 2 racing car of 1969 with the Diametral 1.6-litre competition engine, which brought about a change in BMW's racing fortunes.

ABOVE This Tourist Trophy of the late 1930s included street racing near Belfast. The photo shows how popular the six-cylinder BMW 328 became before the war.

M ost large manufacturers have to think very seriously before they decide to become involved in the expensive business of motoring sport. It is estimated that corporations like Fiat, which owns Ferrari, and Renault, which operates its own competition divisions to tackle Grand Prix racing and World Championship rallying, may spend anywhere between £5 million and £10 million—$9 and $18 million— in pursuit of global glory. But for BMW, competition has always been interwoven with the fabric of company life. And this includes not only motor racing or rallying, but competition in the air, on water or even with two- or three-wheelers. There are more resounding and emotive names in the motor racing world—Ferrari, Lotus and Porsche in particular—yet BMW could justly claim to have been involved in a wider range of motorized competition for longer, and in more variety, than even these prestigious marques.

Since BMW was born of the need for military aero engines, in which the priorities include high performance, light weight and maximum durability, such competitive instincts have always been part of the company's philosophy. There was a number of aerial achievements that continued until the outbreak of World War 2. Some were feats of endurance, others demonstrations of passenger-carrying ability in various German commercial designs. The 1919–39 period brought the company a claimed 98 world records and many other aviation successes. A BMW 12-cylinder aero engine even powered an experimental propeller-driven railway engine, tested between Berlin and Hamburg at 230 km/h (143 mph).

Two-wheel power
BMW entered commercial motorcycle manufacture in 1922: by 1924 the factory was recording competition success, and in 1925 it could already claim 100 racing victories. For motorcycle or, later, sidecar racing, record-breaking and hill-climbing competitions, most of the company's success came when the machines were powered by derivatives of the opposed twin-cylinder *boxer* engines. This was to prove significant in the car world of the late 1950s and early '60s, for the BMW 700 coupés and saloons also used a power unit based on these principles. This BMW flat-twin unit was a rarity in motor sport in providing success on two, three and four wheels.

Although BMW did not become car manufacturers until 1928, the company it took over (Dixi, formerly Wartburg) had a sports prowess that included purpose-built racers for the Grands Prix stretching back to 1900. When BMW became masters at Eisenach, the Dixi 3/15 was a twice-proven competition design: as the Austin Seven in Britain it had a distinguished record; and Dixi had added further success in hill climbs, reliability trials (forerunners of today's high-speed rallies) and racing. Because of BMW's belief in progress through sports, the

factory could not let such an agile little car rest on its laurels. The first major success accredited to BMW came in 1929, and the team was honoured with garlands and a reception at the Eisenach works upon its return. Max Buchner, Albert Kandt and W. Wagner took three BMW 3/15s to the team prize in the 1929 *Alpenpokal*, predecessor of the tough international Alpine Rally. In 1931 there was success in the under-750 cc class in the Monte Carlo Rally and the 3/15 continued to consolidate BMW's reputation at many lesser sporting events.

BMW became a far more serious force in motor sport with the advent of the six-cylinder 315/1. These cars made their début in the 1934 Monte Carlo Rally and went on to take the 1.5-litre class and team prize in the *Alpenpokal* of that year. The 315/1 was also successful under the British Frazer Nash badge, and in races such as 1000-mile events in Czechoslovakia. However, the 1936 début of the 1971 cc BMW 328, with motorcycle ace Ernst Henne at the wheel of one of two such cars made that season, was the point at which BMW started to have a real international impact on motor sport.

As a 2-litre sports racing car the 328 was a most promising contender for class honours wherever it raced: from 1936 until after the war, the 328 won events outright or came first in class all over the world. It was no fragile sprinter either, claiming 2-litre category wins in the 1938 Spa-Francorchamps and the 1939 Le Mans races, both 24-hour events. The most serious factory effort largely went unnoticed, for it was 1940, and wartime, when BMW entered five purpose-built 328 racers for the Mille Miglia. These were very advanced cars, three of them open and two exceptionally streamlined coupés. A very light tubular frame was hidden beneath their aluminium bodies and power was increased from the production 80 bhp to 135. All but one of the BMW 328s completed the 1484 km (922-mile) Mille Miglia, Huschke von Hanstein and Walter Bäumer winning in the Italian-bodied (Touring) 328 at an *average* of over 160 km/h (100 mph) on a closed circuit made up of public roads. The same coupé, which weighed under 650 kg (1433 lb), had also finished fifth at Le Mans the previous year— BMW's best result in the French classic to date.

Haphazard sporting recovery
After the war, as we have seen, simply getting a BMW car into production was difficult, let alone finding the money for a factory competition programme. Privateers, often former personnel who returned to the fold in the 1950s (such as Ernst Loof and Alex von Falkenhausen), used prewar BMW parts from the 328 series in a variety of racing specials that competed in the immediate postwar period. Von Falkenhausen's AFM appeared not only in its creator's hands but also those of legendary 1930s Grand Prix driver Hans

Stuck Snr, and these links would not be forgotten when BMW returned to official competition.

The appearance of Munich-prepared machinery came soon after BMW re-entered car production. Von Falkenhausen, aristocrat and engineer, rejoined the company in 1954 and took on responsibility for the competition activities on two, three and four wheels. This began a tradition of versatility in engineering and competition that has since been carried on by Paul Rosche. As a talented driver, von Falkenhausen had an added incentive to develop the full competition potential of such varied BMWs as the big saloons and the baby Isettas. Indeed, in the 600, with his wife as co-driver, he humbled many potentially more effective rally car mounts, so the 700 was an immediate priority for sports development.

Von Falkenhausen handled the first outing of a works BMW 700 coupé during March 1960. Complete with prominent company insignia and a twin-carburettor version of the 697 cc *boxer* unit, providing perhaps 50 bhp, the car's first competition effort ended when it swallowed a carburettor sealing ring. However, the light weight of engine and car, combined with nimble handling and excellent traction from the rear engine, soon made their mark. Hans

Stuck Snr won the 1960 German National Hill Climb Championship in a BMW 700, the result of many class victories over Abarth-modified Fiats. Even Alfa Romeos of 1.3-litre could frequently be beaten by Hans Stuck, who reportedly enjoyed driving the 50 bhp rear-engined BMW just as much as the 600 bhp leviathans (also rear-engined) of his prewar days with Auto Union. A team of Italian privateers further emphasized the resurgence of BMW by winning a 12-hour race at Monza in 1960 with the 700 coupé.

Through 1961 and 1962 the 700 continued to make competition conquests for the company. It also received a little more power (up to 65 bhp with separate British Amal carburettors) and trained a new generation of drivers who would be vital to BMW. Motorcyclists also provided some of the company's success on four wheels; Walter Schneider won the German national racing title in a 700. Von Falkenhausen himself collected ten class prizes in as many outings, some of them international events such as the 1962 *Coupe de Paris*. By 1963 the speedy little 700 coupés with their Munich registration plates, racing with little more than tuned engines and racing tyres, had become familiar in Britain for their giant-killing activities.

Contemporary German racing pictures show grids of 20 to 30

LEFT *Just one year after the BMW takeover, Max Buchner, Albert Kandt and W. Wagner won the 1929* Alpenpokal *team prize in their BMW 3/15s.*

RIGHT *BMW took first, third, fifth and sixth places in the 1940 Mille Miglia: the 328 of Brudes and Roese, which came third.*

BELOW *BMW 700s raced all over the world in the 1960s; the little racer often put up a spirited display.*

BMW 700s taking the start in national events. Such a popular car made the company many driving friends, including the present-day Alpina-BMW preparation specialist Burkard Bovensiepen; Jacky Ickx, six times Le Mans winner, who distinguished himself by beating the works 700 at Zolder in his private 700 to earn a later BMW driver's contract; and Hubert Hahne. Hahne also beat the factory-prepared 700s in his own car in a 6-hour race at the Nürburgring in 1962, and was employed as a BMW driver in single-seaters and saloons.

Divided loyalties

The 700 gave BMW entrée to competition motoring, but such a small car could not accrue the outright victories the rapidly recovering company aspired to. For BMW the 1960s were characterized by two separate paths towards success: touring car and Formula 2 single-seater racing. The only common ground between the two racing programmes was the immense basic strength of that 1500 four-cylinder production engine. By the close of the decade BMW had scored international victories against the best opposition in both these racing categories, but the road to success had been so rough that the future of *any* factory racing was abruptly curtailed.

Von Falkenhausen and his team began by assessing the opposition within the European Touring Car Championship. This series of long-distance races was then in its infancy: Jaguar had provided the winning car for German Peter Nöcker in the opening season in 1963. The qualifying rounds were long—not less than 3 hours, and up to 24 hours when the Belgian Spa-Francorchamps race joined the series in 1964. Von Falkenhausen knew that sturdy and reliable cars were needed to take the stress of street racing in Budapest or 6 hours around the Nürburgring: but he was also aware how fast and sophisticated the opposition from Alfa Romeo, BMC and Ford had become. Both the latter British companies employed specialists from Grand Prix racing to prepare their saloon racers: Cooper Car Co. for the Mini-Cooper S type and Lotus for the Lotus Cortina. Britain also abounded in specialists like Broadspeed and Alan Mann Racing who transformed 130 km/h (80 mph) family saloons into 192 km/h or 208 km/h (120 or 130 mph) race winners able to lap circuits in times seen in Formula 1 a decade or less before.

Consequently the 1500 BMW was not the right car to succeed: the engine was too small for the capacious and weighty body for sufficient straight-line performance. Instead the factory began its competition preparation with the fundamentally similar 1800, a twin-carburettor 1800 TI providing the basis for a very successful BMW inaugural year in European racing in 1964. In place of the production 110 bhp and just over 160 km/h (100 mph), the small BMW

Competitions Department, then just a preparation area within the main factory, provided 145 to 155 bhp with 'just simple tuning changes', according to von Falkenhausen. Suitable, closer ratios for the four-speed gearbox were provided, along with Koni shock absorbers and stiffer coil springs to provide better roadholding to cope with the car's increased performance, including a maximum speed that could reach 201 km/h (125 mph).

Hahne started 1964 well with a victory in Budapest, and shared the driving for a 12-hour stint around the Nürburgring, which also brought BMW a victory based on durability rather than outright speed. The first outing to the revised Spa 24 hours (it had been an event for sports cars in the 1930s and a natural for BMW 328 success) produced an exceptionally hard-fought second overall for the 1800 TI works car in the hands of Finnish rally star Rauno Aaltonen and Hahne. Their opposition at Spa had included *six* factory-backed cars from Alfa Romeo, a trio of large Mercedes, Alan Mann Lotus Cortinas, and entries from Citroën and Lancia. Throughout the 24 hours the two BMWs fought the Mercedes: the winning works Mercedes averaged 164.8 km/h (102.43 mph) with BMW only fractionally behind at 164.41 km/h (102.16 mph). It had been a thrilling encounter around the closed public roads of the Ardennes Forest, but the team members knew that they needed more power and better cornering if they were to win regularly. However, the 1800 TI did an admirable job, netting another European Championship race victory at Zandvoort, Holland, plus the German national title for Hubert Hahne. 'Hubie's' driving style was to slide the car so much that onlookers were surprised that he could finish one lap, let alone survive several hours' racing.

For 1965 BMW was equipped with a more sophisticated touring car: the 1800 TI/SA. This machine was 20 kg (44 lb) lighter than the 1800 TI, offered up to 165 bhp from its Weber twin-carb. engine, and had refinements such as wider wheels (6 in × 14), anti-roll bars front and rear to improve cornering, and a maximum speed in the 204–211 km/h (127–130 mph) region. There was also a five-speed gearbox from Getrag, the first on a postwar BMW. Yet the cars had a miserable season with only one significant highlight. BMW entered five grey TI/SAs for the Spa 24 hours and was rewarded with Pascal Ickx (the brother of Jacky) and G. Langlois van Ophem winning outright. In rainy conditions their average speed was less than the previous year and the four other works cars all retired with mechanical failures: persistent overheating was a common problem despite detuned engines.

The 1800 TI/SA carried on as the factory racer until July 1966, when it was replaced by the 2000 TI. This was much the same car, but with a 2-litre engine, capable of generating 170 bhp in

competition trim. That was just in time for the Spa event, where Jacky Ickx set the fastest practice time against a Ford Mustang V8 which had twice the BMW's engine capacity. This was an astonishing feat on such a fast track. Ickx and Hahne shared one of only two works cars entered and duly won the race at a record 168.66 km/h (104.8 mph) average. That season Hahne was one of three champions in the three-class European Championship.

1967: all change

Although saloon cars were getting more and more like racing cars, they could still be driven to and from meetings, and a faction within BMW felt they must establish the company's credentials in proper single-seater racing. Working within the BMW engineering department of the mid-1960s was Ludwig Apfelbeck, designer of motorcycle speedway engines. The department experimented with an Apfelbeck radial valve single-cylinder engine and found it gave an exceptional output. Unfortunately, what works on the test bed does not always work when installed in a car, particularly when the radial valve design, with its inherent complexity, had to be scaled up to sit on the BMW 1500 four-cylinder block. Because the valves were radially positioned, four per cylinder, a total of eight carburettors and a similar number of primary exhaust pipes had to be plumbed around the ungainly motor. Initial trials in 2-litre form, where it did not have to rev as highly as was needed for a 1.6-litre Formula 2 application, took place in a 1965 Brabham. Hahne won a local hill climb, and von Falkenhausen adapted the unit to run on nitromethane for the short burst of record runs when an astonishing 330 bhp was measured.

During the winter of 1966–7 the decision was taken to proceed further with this engine in 1.6-litre Formula 2 form, when it would have Lucas fuel injection and develop some 225 bhp at a damaging 10,500 rpm. Touring cars could wait while a series of British Lola chassis was adapted to the BMW engine: one two-car team was run by John Surtees in England and the other from Munich, with the rapid Swiss Jo Siffert and BMW's own Hubert Hahne driving. The first two races were held in Britain over the Easter weekend and were a fiasco. The rival Cosworth Ford FVA 1600 proved itself despite a theoretical power disadvantage, while the radial-valve Apfelbeck BMW demonstrated the valve gear unreliability that was to haunt it as long as it was expected to rev at 10,000 rpm. When the cars appeared at the Nürburgring in 1967, BMW's directors were so appalled by their performance that they asked for them to be withdrawn after practice! However, finally the cars were allowed to take part in the race.

By the end of 1967 BMW's position in Formula 2 was not encouraging, but the 2-litre engine in a Lola T110 sports racer (badged as BMW 2000!) provided the factory's new Austrian driving

During 1967 and 1968 BMW developed an effective combination for European hill-climbing: a Lola sports car chassis with the 2-litre engine designed by Ludwig Apfelbeck. The Monti Bergspyder *version is seen here.*

recruit Dieter Quester with a number of top five positions in the European Hill Climb Championship; he finished fourth overall in the series. The following year Quester raced an adapted Lola-Apfelbeck BMW, as well as using a more radically modified version on the same theme for hill-climbing under the name *Monti Bergspyder*. The hill-climbing activity went well and the ugly sports-racer mongrel took four second places in a year dominated by a factory Porsche in the European Championship. The 2-litre version of the engine was also permitted an annual appearance at the German GP from 1967 to '69, when it performed reliably in the hands of David Hobbs or Hahne.

Autumn 1968 saw BMW's persistence in Formula 2 producing a ray of hope. A new Lola chassis, the T102, had been produced and the engine had the redesigned Diametral cylinder head. This retained three sparkplugs per cylinder and four valves, but these valves were placed with the inlets and exhausts diametrically opposed to each other. The fuel-injected engine looked much neater than the Apfelbeck, and was still claimed to offer a peak power advantage over the Cosworth FVA, but there were to be no top three finishing positions in 1968.

During 1968 and into 1969 the competitions team, now with a full-time manager because of von Falkenhausen's increasing engineering work load, experimented with the fashionable large rear wings on stilts that had increased cornering ability so rapidly in Formula 1 cars, but which also proved very fragile when they reached extreme heights. The factory also experimented with the installation of sidepods to try and improve straight-line speed, for early in 1969 BMW had been robbed of one win by just 0.61 seconds. During that season the Englishman Len Terry designed a new chassis and body for Dornier to build at its famous aircraft factory north of Munich. The new monocoque chassis (the BMW 269) ran in the third round of the 1969 European Championship; and fuel injection from Kugelfischer replaced the Lucas system a race later. All the time the cars were becoming more competitive and getting over their original problems, but tragedy was in store. Hahne broke his foot in a pre-race crash at Enna Pergusa in Sicily that put him out of contention for the European title; and the revered former hill-climb champion Gerhard Mitter was killed in August at the Nürburgring.

Hahne finished the year as runner-up in the European Formula 2 series and there was considerable discussion among the BMW directors before they allowed the single-seater programme to continue, for 1968 and 1969 had seen increasing success with the 2002 touring cars in Europe.

However, it was left to Alpina to prepare BMWs to defend Munich's touring car honour and the factory BMW 269/270 Dornier single-seater designs with the Diametral engines showed their worth with five international Formula 2 victories in 1969 and a stack of top three placings. The Dornier-BMW liaison and the Diametral engine were now working, but even so in August 1970 Jacky Ickx gave a third and final BMW racing 16-valve engine its début. This parallel valve unit, using much the same principles as Cosworth had exploited, did not provide the same ultimate power as its predecessor had shown on the test bed, but it won races from the start and gave the drivers

RIGHT *In 1969 the fast Hockenheim circuit provided BMW with hope for its Formula 2 programme. Hubert Hahne (seen here) scored two second places in traditional slip-streaming manner that season.*

BMW 2002 TIK racing saloon (1969)	
ENGINE	
No. of cylinders	4, in-line
Bore/stroke mm	89 × 80
Displacement cc	1990
Valve operation	Chain-driven single overhead camshaft, two valves per cylinder
Compression ratio	Reduced from 8.5:1 to below 7:1 in racing life
Induction	Kugelfischer mechanical fuel injection and single KKK turbocharger
BHP	270–290 at 7200 rpm with 1.0 to 1.2 atm boost pressure
DRIVE TRAIN	
Clutch	Single plate
Transmission	Getrag 5-speed gearbox
CHASSIS	
Frame	Unitary steel with pop-riveted lightweight panels
Weight kg	860
Wheelbase mm	2500
Track – front mm	Approx 1418
Track – rear mm	Approx 1470
Suspension – front	Modified MacPherson struts, Koni damping; anti-roll bar choice
Suspension – rear	Semi-trailing arms, Koni damping, shorter and stiffer coil springs
Brakes	2000-series 272 mm disc (front) and 2002 256 mm disc (rear)
Tyres	Dunlop racing
Wheels	BBS split rim aluminium with cast alloy centres: 13-inch diameter; 8-inch wide (front), 10-inch (rear)
PERFORMANCE	
Maximum speed	250 km/h (155 mph)
Acceleration	0–100 km/h (62 mph) 6 sec or less
Number built	No more than 4

RIGHT *The start of the 1969 Brands Hatch 6-hours, and battle is already joined between the BMW 2002 TIK (left) and the works Ford Escorts. On this occasion BMW won— fractionally!*

much more usable power throughout the rev range. This lesson of usable power was one BMW had to re-establish with the 1980s' Grand Prix unit . . .

Roofed prowess

While BMW was having problems with single-seaters, its return to touring car racing with the 2002 models was a spectacular success. BMW scored four outright European Championship victories in 1968, including a one-two result at home at the Nürburgring 6 hours. The cars now developed 180 bhp on Weber carburettors and 210 bhp with Kugelfischer injection, like the system used in Formula 2. The racing 2002 was much lighter than its four-door predecessors, at 890 kg (1962 lb) and used anything up to 10 in wide wheels under a body modified with aluminium and glass-fibre weight-saving parts.

The 1968 season brought BMW a European title under the three-class system and Dieter Quester a driver's championship, but BMW saved its spectacular effort for 1969. During 1968 the factory had found it hard to beat the Porsche 911s that were then allowed in saloon car racing (they have since been banned for lack of internal passenger space!), so von Falkenhausen's team rapidly produced the first European turbocharged racing saloon. Equipped with a

Kühnle, Köpp and Kausch (KKK) turbocharger, the production-based 1990 cc engine gave up to 290 bhp and 250 km/h (155 mph)! Such a sharp power boost developed so quickly was not completely reliable, but the turbocharged 2002 tii was able to achieve four outright victories that season, one a dramatic last-ditch affair at Brands Hatch, and maintain both BMW and Quester as supreme in their division of the 1969 Championship, Porsche or no Porsche!

At this point BMW handed over its touring car racing activities to Alpina at Buchloe, west of Munich. This specialist Bavarian company not only developed the 1602 and 2002 (in non-turbocharged form) as consistent championship point collectors, but also scored the first European Championship win for the six-cylinder 2800 CS coupé, at the Salzburgring in Austria, on 12 April 1970.

On 20 October that year the managing board of BMW announced a complete withdrawal from competition motoring. It was emphasized that the four Formula 2 cars, now firm favourites for the 1971 European Championship, plus their 12 engines, would *not* be for sale to privateers.

Could this really be the end? BMW certainly had enough on its plate keeping up with public demand for the road cars, as we shall see in the following chapter.

FROM RENAISSANCE TO PROSPERITY

Although four-cylinder cars had powered the BMW renaissance of the 1960s the company was not likely to forget its tradition of in-line 6-cylinder units when there was the finance to expand the range of cars further. The year 1968 was the most important in BMW's recovery and the link between the BMW of old and the expanding and prosperous company of the 1980s. Within those 12 months many plans at BMW were realized, including the manufacture of over 100,000 cars in a year, the continued transfer of motorcycle production to Berlin; the renovation of the Glas factory at Dingolfing to suit BMW needs (of today's major models only the 3-series is made in Munich); and the unveiling in September 1968 of that long-awaited six-cylinder model.

BMW's rapidly increasing wealth was reflected in the stylish press launch at the Tegernsee lakeside of not just one six-cylinder saloon but three new models available in coupé (CS) two-door or four-door saloon bodies. Developed under the overall control of Bernhard Osswald, engineering director from 1965 to 1975, the big new BMWs amounted to an expansion of the basic principles found in the four-cylinder range. The single overhead camshaft was chain driven and operated the aluminium cylinder head's inlet and exhaust valves in the same V-arrangement with BMW's unique combustion chamber shape. The smaller 2494 cc six that was installed in the 2500 saloon, and in the much later economy model, the 2.5 CS of 1974–5, had much the same short-stroke proportions as the four-cylinder engine, 71.6 mm, only fractionally more than on the original 1500 saloon and the later 1600 and 1600-2 designs. The bore of the 2.5-litre unit was some 2 mm longer than in the previous 1800 and 3 mm shorter than the widely used 2-litre engine of the 2000, 2002, and 2000 CS.

At that 1968 launch the new BMW 2.5-litre six appeared only in saloon form, although it subsequently did stout work in many other BMW designs. In addition the 2500 proved the longest-lived of the original 1968 saloons in production terms, being offered until 1977 in much the same 150 bhp form. The larger 2.8-litre engine also shared the basic BMW principles of overhead camshaft, alloy cylinder head and an iron cylinder block 30° from vertical; with its extra 20 bhp it was installed in the sporting 2800 CS as well as the 2800 saloon. The 2788 cc capacity was achieved by the alliance of the 2.5-litre's 86 mm cylinder bore and the same 80 mm stroke as used in the 2-litre four-cylinder unit. The result was so successful it has been described by many experts as the world's best six-cylinder unit. The engine remained in continuous production for the next 14 years, and fuel injection versions appear in today's 5-, 6- and 7-series. (For details on these cars, see pages 59–67.)

The six-cylinder units were to prove powerful and reliable in the best BMW traditions—but what of the other features of the new design? Again the basics were retained from four-cylinder experience, but precious little was carried over into the new saloons; the coupés were a different matter and a large proportion of older bodywork and running gear could be found on these.

The saloons were built on a 2692 mm (106 in) wheelbase, whereas the previous four-cylinder four-doors, and the 2000 C/CS, had been constructed on a 2550 mm (100 in) base. The saloons were the biggest BMWs seen since the eight-cylinder range of the 1950s and early '60s, measuring 4700 mm (185 in) long and 1750 mm (69 in) wide, with an overall height of 1450 mm (57 in). These measurements were not far short of those earlier elaborate eights, although most comparisons concerned the similarity in size and engine capacity of these latest saloons and the 'New Generation' Mercedes. Generally the BMW came out with a reputation for unmatched performance with a notably smooth power delivery, and a firmer ride with sportier handling than Mercedes was able to offer. However, many criticisms were levelled that BMW could not match the sheer quality in assembly and basic engineering of Mercedes.

It was therefore a pity that the more luxury equipment was supplied for the earlier 2800s, the more their owners complained! The ZF automatic transmission was not loved for its durability and the production four-speed manual gearbox was extensively revised to overcome a weakness in the synchromesh that was particularly noticeable when engaging second gear rapidly. By April 1971 a new set of ratios for second and third was substituted. Other production changes concerned the carburation (the 2500 did not receive an automatic choke until 1973) and the deletion of limited-slip differential and Boge self-levelling devices from the standard production specification of the 2800 saloon.

The underpinnings

Underneath their shiny new bodies the 2800 CS and 2800 saloon shared engine, gearbox and rear end transmission through differential and halfshafts, but the running gear to support the 170 bhp sixes in their respective two- and four-door bodywork was very different. The 2800 CS ran on the shorter 2625 mm (103 in) wheelbase that owed most to the 2000 C/CS and therefore to the generation of four-door saloons that had founded BMW's recovery. Worthy as those had been, they were not the best base for a new six-cylinder coupé of sporting inclinations, a fact reflected in the use of drum brakes at the rear of the CS, while the saloon had a new four-wheel disc braking system.

The suspension principles that BMW has used since the 1500 (but with a significant number of modifications over the years to keep pace with improved tyres and higher customer expectations) were retained in the new sixes. MacPherson strut front suspension was used with trailing arm rear. This was an all-independent layout that featured an optional front roll bar for the saloons until 1971, when it became a production item, although it had been standard from the start on the CS. In the same way power steering was a production item on the CS while it was an option for both saloons.

Although the saloons were obviously brand-new designs as far as their bodywork was concerned, the 2800 CS reflected its mixed ancestry behind its similar quadruple-headlamp front. In fact, only half the CS was new. From the front windscreen to the rear it was fundamentally the old 2000 C/CS, including the basic floorpan. Forward of the windscreen new sheet metal gave an increase in overall length together with a slight enlargement in wheelbase. This accommodated the front suspension and disc braking of the saloon, together with an engine that could produce 70 bhp more than the 2000 C and 50 bhp more than the original twin-carburettor 2000 CS. The bodies for the CS models continued to be made at the north German factory of Karmann, then best known for convertible and coupé Volkswagen coachwork.

High performance

Although the new engines had to haul 1360 kg (2992 lb) in the saloons and 1355 kg (2981 lb) in the 2800 CS, none of the cars could be described as slow, even by the standards of today. The 2800 saloon could exceed 200 km/h (124 mph) and reach 100 km/h (62 mph) from rest in 10 seconds, the acceleration standard that many motorists used to divide the really sporty cars from the pretenders. Yet BMW was providing such performance in an

BMW 2500 (1968–77)			
ENGINE		**CHASSIS**	
No. of cylinders	6, in-line	Frame	Unitary steel, 4 doors
Bore/stroke mm	86 × 71.6	Weight kg	1360 (automatic model 1380)
Displacement cc	2494		
Valve operation	Chain-driven single overhead camshaft	Wheelbase mm	2692
		Track – front mm	1446
Compression ratio	9:1	Track – rear mm	1464
Induction	Two downdraught Zenith 35/40 carburettors. From Sept '73, Zenith 32/40 carburettors with automatic chokes	Suspension – front	MacPherson struts; anti-roll bar from 1971
		Suspension – rear	Semi-trailing arms, coil springs; Boge Nivomat self-levelling device and anti-roll bar from 1971
BHP	150 at 6000 rpm		
Torque	212 Nm (156 lbf. ft) at 3700 rpm	Brakes	Servo-assisted 4-wheel disc brakes of 272 mm diameter
DRIVE TRAIN		Tyre size	175 HR 14
Clutch	Single dry plate, hydraulic operation	Wheels	6J 14 H2 pressed steel
Transmission	4-speed all-synchromesh gearbox to split propshaft and via differential and halfshafts to rear wheels	**PERFORMANCE**	
		Maximum speed	190 km/h (118 mph)
		Acceleration	0–100 km/h (62 mph) 11 sec
		Fuel consumption	16 litres/100 km (17.66 mpg)
		Number built	94,207

PRECEDING PAGES *This beautiful 1974 BMW 3.0 CSi is typical of the cars that were seen on British roads during the mid-1970s, and were similar in appearance to the UK market CSLs. Fuel injection gave them a smooth 210 km/h (130 mph). Provided by Mrs H. Gates.*

RIGHT *The 2500 saloon eventually shared all but its engine size with the 2800. Both were well-bred, roomy vehicles that took BMW back into the big-car market. The 2500 saloon remained in production from 1968 to 1977. Provided by L&C Auto Services.*

At rest or at speed the lightweight version of the BMW coupé made an arresting sight with the 'Batmobile' racing wing kit erected. Three engine capacities were used on the cars badged 3.0 CSL: this is the final 3153 cc model. These original CSLs, capable of 220 km/h (137 mph), are now quite rare. Provided by L&C Auto Services.

ostensibly upright saloon with plenty of luggage space and accommodation. Even the less powerful 2500 was expected to provide 190 km/h (118 mph) and reach 100 km/h only a second after its big brother; the 2800 CS was credited with a 206 km/h (128 mph) maximum speed and was also capable of accelerating from 0 to 100 km/h in 10 seconds.

Fuel consumption was estimated at between 16 and 16.5 litres/100 km (17.7 and 17.1 mpg) under the worst conditions the factory could manage, but many owners stayed happily between 13.5 and 14.9 litres/100 km (21 and 19 mpg).

The new sixes were well received, but BMW was almost embarrassed by demand, making only 140 of the 2800 saloons in 1968, and also failing to contain the lengthening waiting lists with the manufacture of 2560 of the smaller-engined saloons that same year. By 1969 all BMW motorcycles were manufactured in Berlin.

However, 1969 saw BMW set new company records, including the output of just over 20,000 BMW 2500s and 16,611 2800 saloons. That year the company employed more than 20,000 people for the first time since the wartime peak of 42,346 in 1942, and overall car production reached nearly 150,000. Such rapid progress, aided by increasing export sales, has been the hallmark of BMW virtually ever since. By 1980, BMW AG in Munich employed 37,246 and was making 341,031 cars annually. The following year the home workforce was increased by 7 per cent to 39,777, and 351,545 cars and 33,120 motorcycles were produced, the latter a 13.2 per cent increase at a time when Japanese competition could not have been stiffer. In 1980 around 58 per cent of BMW cars were exported, and the figure was 60 per cent or 210,547 cars in 1981. That

employment peak of 1942 had been surpassed by the 1980s for, if you include operations around the world, such as BMW North America and BMW Great Britain, total company employment had reached 44,648 during 1981.

The 1968 six-cylinder range contributed a great deal to the company's turnover, total production of the various types reaching 252,559, including 44,254 coupés. However, it was not all glittering success, particularly in America where, from the 1969 introduction of the six-cylinder saloon, sales proved rather lethargic. By 1971 BMW had dealt with this problem by introducing the Bavaria, a cocktail of cheaper 2500 equipment and the 2800 engine. The 1971 Bavaria even had a European-style power output and the nameplate was carried on to its 3-litre carburated and fuel-injected successors, which stayed on the American market until 1975. In fact, you can see the big chrome Bavaria boot badges on an enormous variety of vehicles in and around Munich to this day.

In Europe development of the six-cylinder saloons followed logical lines but they were given the usual baffling system of numbers and suffixes. BMW and Mercedes excel at this arcane badgework, although BMW did return to more logical designations after the demise of the large six-cylinder saloons in 1977.

The 2500 had the simplest production record, running from 1968 to 1977 with the few minor changes already noted. The 2800 remained officially in production until 1974, but was continued in the guise of the 2.8 L of 1975–7. The L stood for *lang* and referred to the long wheelbase, which was extended by 100 mm (4 in) to give a total of 2792 mm (110 in). Like Jaguar and Mercedes, BMW had concentrated the extra length behind the centre pillar to the benefit

of the rear passengers and to the detriment of kerb weight, which went up by 80 kg (176 lb). Long wheelbase examples of the saloon subsequently included two 3.3-litre models: the 3.3 L of 1974–6 with 190 bhp from the 3295 cc engine, and the 3.3 L fuel-injected version of 1976–7, which developed 196 bhp from a marginally shorter-stroke version of the rugged 3210 cc six. Such slight changes in engine capacity do occur repeatedly in BMW history—in 1982 just such an adjustment was made to the 635 CSi, and the 1800 had two engines during the 1960s. These alterations brought an even sweeter-running unit with the bonus of reliability and ease of production for customer and factory alike: yet the basic principles of the engines remained unchanged; they were merely refined and developed over the years.

Although the 2800 was still being made in 1974 on the normal wheelbase, it had truly been supplanted by the 180 bhp 3.0 S; in this case the S stood for Saloon, although Sport might have been appropriate because of the extra 10 bhp. The 3-litre version of the six was ready for the German market in April 1971, and immediately revived the popularity of the bigger-engined BMW saloon. Yet it was soon outshone by the definitive 3-litre BMW six, the 3.0 Si of September of that same year! The fuel injection system on the Si was by Bosch, as always on BMW six-cylinder power units (Kugelfischer mechanical injection systems were used in the four-cylinder power plants from 1969 to '75), yet two different Bosch systems were utilized for the 3.0 Si. Originally the engine was rated at 200 bhp and

ran a 9.5:1 compression ratio with Bosch D-Jetronic injection. From September 1976 the compression was lowered slightly to 9:1, the injection system updated to Bosch L-Jetronic, but the power dropped to 195 bhp. Similarly the maximum torque figure was also slightly amended, but with over 265 Nm (195 lbf. ft) there was plenty of pulling power available in either version.

The 210 km/h (130 mph) 3.0 Si was a superb four-door saloon that had vigour, balanced by four-wheel ventilated disc brakes, and a turn of speed that continued to surprise right up to the end of its production life in 1977. In production form the 3.0 Si could sprint from rest to 100 km/h (62 mph) in only 8.5 seconds, but that kind of action could also reduce fuel economy to 17.5 litres/100 km (16.1 mpg)!

Coupé: towards a racing base
Development of the 2800 CS ran parallel to the saloons, although production did not begin until December 1968. The 3-litre carburettor and Bosch electronic fuel injection versions of the engines arrived in 1971, accompanied by a welcome conversion to four-wheel disc brakes, which made the CS series safer. Because of the coupé's 20 mm (¾ in) narrower body and 80 mm (3 in) lower roofline, BMW always claimed it had a better performance than the saloon equivalents, resulting in an estimated maximum speed of 220 km/h (137 mph) for the 3.0 CSi.

Now the 3-litre CS machines were the fastest BMWs in the range, it was not long before the legendary series of special coupés began to make an appearance under the generic CSL badge. This time the L stood for *leichtgewicht* (lightweight), which referred to a specially made Karmann coupé bodyshell. It utilized alloy skins instead of steel for components like doors, boot and bonnet to reduce weight from the standard 1400 kg (3080 lb) to 1200 kg (2640 lb) in the original carburated model of May 1971, or 1270 kg (2794 lb) in the more common fuel-injected CSL versions that ceased production in 1975. The object of this reduction was to increase competitiveness in saloon car racing, and this aim also produced the subsequent official engine sizes of 3003 and 3153 cc as well as the original carburated 2985 cc. The 3.2-litre unit allowed BMW to use up to 3.5 litres in racing and, together with the celebrated 'Batmobile' wing set, enabled the company to trounce its rivals Ford in the 1973 European Touring Car Championship, a story that is included in the next chapter.

For the public, the CSL road cars that had to be made to support that racing effort became valuable collector's items, although it should be noted that at least 500 of the cars exported to Britain were in a luxurious specification that made a mockery of the lightweight suffix. However, a 3.2-litre CSL of the 1973–5 period made a formidable mileage-eater, capable of close on 225 km/h (140 mph). During independent tests in Britain it dashed from 0–60 mph in a little over 7 seconds.

Turbo pioneer

The four-cylinder 02 models of the late 1960s provided a base on which to expand into the following decade: six cylinders may have had glamour and speed, but BMW's fours proved appealing in balancing sport with affordable economy. Thus the 02 derivatives continued to multiply with astonishing speed. Using engines of 1600, 1800 or 2000 cc, BMW built new bodies on that 02 basis, including the 1971–4 hatchback Touring models and a series of convertibles produced by Baur at Stuttgart from 1971 to '75. Engine power of the slant fours could be anything the customer demanded between the 75 bhp of the economy conscious 1975–7 1502 and the 170 bhp of the ill-fated 1973–4 2002 turbo. This aggressive 211 km/h (131 mph) BMW appeared in the fuel crisis years and contributed to a public

LEFT *The 2002 Turbo was introduced in 1974, after the onset of the fuel crisis, and pioneered European saloon car use of the now ubiquitous turbocharger. Rather unrefined, but able to achieve 211 km/h (131 mph), the 2002 Turbo was the most powerful 02 series.*

BELOW *BMW has a habit of making the most exciting production models available right at the end of their manufacturing run. Here is the 218 bhp 1981 M535i, which saw out production of the original 5-series: 2.8 litres was the maximum of the new series in 1983.*

outcry against performance cars in Germany. In fact the 2002 turbo deserved a better production run than the 1670 examples recorded, for it was a landmark not only in BMW's history as the company's first turbocharged road car, but it was also Europe's first production turbo to be offered to the public. If you remember that everyone from Renault to Porsche now offers such exhaust-driven turbines to enhance the performance and image of their wares, you can see BMW paid a very high price indeed for pioneering. This 2002 special, with its stripy body, was immensely fast, its 2 litres of KKK turbocharged power producing 0–100 km/h (62 mph) figures of around 8 seconds or less and also gave owners the opportunity to cruise at 190 km/h (120 mph) alongside the disconcerted drivers of larger BMWs and Mercedes—at least for the rather short life of the turbocharger. The car is now rated highly by collectors, but it had no motor sport pedigree.

A far more significant year in BMW history was 1972. In the year that Munich was host city to the Olympic Games, BMW displayed its spectacular 'four-cylinder' office block and adjacent eggcup-styled museum. In September 1972 BMW also had a new four-door car to offer faithful customers of the previous 2000, together with a new numbering system that persists to this day. Under the control of current chairman Eberhard von Kuenheim (appointed from an industrial engineering background in 1970), BMW began to reveal the path it would follow to success, and the straightforward styling of the initial models, the four-cylinder 520 and its Kugelfischer injected brother the 520i, reflected this exactly.

Built on a 2636 mm (104 in) wheelbase with an overall length of 4620 mm (182 in) the 5-series cars have proved among the most versatile and most enduring of BMW designs. Retaining the MacPherson strut and trailing arm independent suspension, with adequate room for four adults, this series has catered perfectly for middle class families all over the world in an amazing variety of power and equipment guises. Even though the 5-series was extensively revised with a far more aerodynamic body of 2625 mm (103 in) wheelbase in June 1981, its appearance has altered little in more than a decade of production, which included over 700,000 of the original series.

BMW played the power and options game with a vengeance on the 5-series, which also established the family look BMWs carry today. The 520 lasted with four-cylinder power (and a subsequent insertion of Bosch fuel injection for the 520i) until 1977, when it inherited one of the new generation of small M60 six-cylinder engines that had been designed for the smaller 3-series. That engine, but with Bosch mechanical K-Jetronic injection, lives on in the 1980s' version of the 520i.

In September 1973 the 2.5-litre six of 2500 saloon fame became a 5-series alternative, and that too lived on in fuel injection form for the 1982 model range, badged as 525i and resplendent with the

BMW 520i (1981–)

ENGINE

No. of cylinders	6, in-line
Bore/stroke mm	80 × 66
Displacement cc	1990
Valve operation	Belt-driven single overhead camshaft
Compression ratio	9.8:1
Induction	Bosch K-Jetronic mechanical fuel injection
BHP	125 at 5800 rpm
Torque	166 Nm (122 lbf. ft) at 4500 rpm

DRIVE TRAIN

Clutch	Single dry plate, membrane spring, hydraulic operation
Transmission	4-speed all-synchromesh or optional 5-speed, or 3-speed ZF automatic gearbox; propshaft to differential and rear halfshafts

CHASSIS

Frame	Unitary steel, 4 doors
Weight kg	1220
Wheelbase mm	2625
Track – front mm	1430
Track – rear mm	1470
Suspension – front	MacPherson struts, coil springs, anti-roll bar, anti-dive compensation
Suspension – rear	Semi-trailing arms, coil springs, anti-dive compensation
Brakes	Discs (front) 284 mm diameter; drums (rear) 250 mm diameter
Tyre size	175 HR 14
Wheels	5½J × 14 H2 pressed steel with alloy option

PERFORMANCE

Maximum speed	185 km/h (115 mph)
Acceleration	0–100 km/h (62 mph) in 11.8 sec
Fuel consumption	12.5 litres/100 km (22.96 mpg)
Number built	From 1972 to introduction of new series in June 1981 over 700,000 5-series built

four-wheel disc brakes that used to be reserved for the 528 of 1975. In August 1977, the 528 became the 528i with Bosch L-Jetronic injection, 176 bhp and a maximum speed of 208 km/h (129 mph).

There had always been a limited number of BMW Motorsport GmbH 3- and 3.3-litre specials made to satisfy more enthusiastic customers (although the 530i was both an American and South African production reality), but BMW made perhaps the finest ever 5-series car by inserting the 3.5-litre 218 bhp six and uprating both suspension and braking for the M-for-Motorsport M535i in 1980–1.

Unfortunately the 225 km/h (140 mph) 535 was not carried over to the revised 1981 models, but the basic 518 of 1974 vintage was still represented in the 90 bhp and 1766 cc four-cylinder trim: it was the only new 5-series without fuel injection in a line-up that read 518, 520i, 525i and the now 184 bhp/209 km/h (130 mph) 528i. The later 5-series cars combined an admirable improvement in both performance and economy, plus the pioneering use of the electronic Service Interval Indicator to replace fixed maintenance mileage.

The smallest BMW grows
The next débutant in BMW's current range was the 3-series, the smallest car from Munich today. Production started on 2 May 1975 and German sales began in August 1975. Right-hand drive cars were available by October of that year. Once more the basics of a single overhead camshaft engine, with trailing arm rear-wheel drive, plus MacPherson strut front suspension, were adhered to. However, there were important changes, such as the use of rack and pinion steering in place of the worm and roller layout BMW had used in all its four-cylinder cars since the original 1500. BMW also made no secret of the fact that the 3-series had been designed with the forthcoming small six-cylinder engine in mind. Thus initial criticism of the size and weight of the 3-series when compared to the 02 did not bother BMW unduly. Yet Anglo-German reaction to the rather soft initial suspension settings did result in a crisper response from the chassis by the time the six-cylinder 320 and 323i arrived in August 1977 (the following year for Britain).

Compared with the 02s the 3-series cars were built on a 63 mm (2½ in) longer wheelbase and were also longer overall and wider, although the height was the same. The 2002 was also 90 kg (190 lb) lighter than the similarly engined 320. Therefore it was quite a relief to BMW when the two M60-coded sixes became available, with their belt-driven overhead camshafts. The 2-litre M60 was a very over-square 80 × 66 mm design providing 122 bhp with one Solex carburettor. The 2315 cc M60 engine simply had a longer stroke (76.8 mm) and Bosch K-Jetronic injection allied to electronic ignition, sharing the 30° slant installation of all modern BMWs, except that exotic mid-engined M1 (see next chapter).

The 143 bhp 323i had the task of upholding the BMW reputation for smaller sporty cars, heading the range with a 192 km/h (119 mph)

ABOVE *The four-door 3-series BMW was to follow the two-door, 139 bhp 323i (inset) into production in 1983. The new two-door 3-series was available in Germany at the end of 1982 and signified a general refinement in handling and in noise levels, and the increasing use of electronics: a Service Interval Indicator replaced fixed service mileages, and an optional computer was available. All new 3-series cars have revised rear suspension and widespread use of fuel injection.*

LEFT *The BMW 3-series Cabriolets were built by Baur of Stuttgart. Expensive but well-executed, these soft-top cars were made in 1.6-, 2.0- or 2.3-litre form. A 1982 320 provided by Romans of Farnborough.*

performance with acceleration similar to that of the 1969 2002 tii. At the other end of the scale was the 1563 cc BMW 316 which could touch 161 km/h (100 mph) only under favourable circumstances, but could provide up to 9.42 litres/100 km (30 mpg); the 316 was the only model with two headlamps, the others having four. (BMW badge logic breaks down occasionally on the 3-series: the present UK 316 has the 1.8-litre engine while the American 320 actually has a fuel-injected 1.8-litre four-cylinder unit.)

BMW's concept of a more comfortable yet still sporty small car was a tremendous success. Always a top contender in Germany, the 3-series had sold an astonishing 1,527,256 examples from the 1975 début to the end of 1981. By autumn 1982 BMW had prepared a new body with revised aerodynamics, reminiscent of the 5-series modifications of June 1981. A two-door version was offered from November 1982 with a four-door model in 1983.

Today's big BMWs
Almost too similar in looks for sales comfort, the big BMWs that top today's prestige offerings from Munich were introduced separately. The two-door 630 and 633 CSi of March 1976 rested on the 2625 mm (103 in) wheelbase used for the previous CS cars, but the 6-series actually owes much of its running gear and floorpan to the 5-series. This is particularly true today where the latest 5- and 6-series share the same wheelbase. However, in the cause of style, the 6-series is 135 mm (5 in) longer and appreciably lower than the four-door 5s.

The 6-series lacked some of the sporting panache of its predecessors, so in July 1978 the 218 bhp six of 3453 cc was installed in the BMW 635 CSi, to provide 222 km/h (138 mph) and 0–100 km/h (62 mph) sprint performance of 8 seconds. From July 1982, by which time BMW was able to report 'approximately 35,000 vehicles of this series have rolled off the assembly lines', the company offered Europeans the choice of the 2788 cc 628 CSi of 212 km/h (132 mph) capability, or a new 3430 cc version of the fabled straight six. The latter was still known as the 635 CSi but was a very much more economical and refined car with many of the electronic features of the revised 5-series. Power output remained at the same quoted level, but weight was down by a claimed 60 kg (132 lb) and the aerodynamics slightly modified. *Autocar* carried out an independent test on the car that showed a 227 km/h (141 mph) maximum speed, 0–100 km/h (62 mph) in a startling 7.3 seconds, and a fine 12.95 litres/100 km (21.8 mpg) overall, including the rigours of performance testing. However, the total list price in the UK was over £23,000 by then.

The biggest BMWs offered today, the 2795 mm (110 in) wheelbase 7-series, went into German production in May 1977 to supersede the 3.0 range. By December 1981 some 129,804 7-series cars had been made, including the original carburated 728 and 730, plus the 3210 cc 733 CSi model that topped the range until the arrival in July 1979 of the lighter (by up to 70 kg, 154 lb) 728i, 732i, 735i and the left-hand-drive only 745i. Now all the models in the 7-series had

BMW 635 CSi (1978–)

(Figures given first refer to the mid-1982 model)

ENGINE

No. of cylinders	6, in-line
Bore/stroke mm	92 × 86 (originally 93.4 × 84)
Displacement cc	3430 (originally 3453)
Valve operation	Chain-driven single overhead camshaft
Compression ratio	10:1 (originally 9.5:1)
Induction	Bosch electronic fuel injection
BHP	218 at 5200 rpm
Torque	311 Nm (229 lbf. ft) at 4000 rpm

DRIVE TRAIN

Clutch	Single dry plate, hydraulic operation
Transmission	Choice of 5-speed manual or 3-speed automatic gearbox

CHASSIS

Frame	Unitary steel, 2-door
Weight kg	1430 (originally 1475)
Wheelbase mm	2626
Track – front mm	1430 (originally 1422)
Track – rear mm	1460 (originally 1487)
Suspension – front	MacPherson struts, coil springs, anti-roll bar
Suspension – rear	Semi-trailing arms, coil springs, anti-roll bar
Brakes	4-wheel disc, 280 mm diameter (front) and 272 mm (rear)
Tyre size	205/70 VR 14 or TRX option (originally 195/70 VR 14)
Wheels	6½J × 14 A1 alloy BBS Mahle

PERFORMANCE

Maximum speed	229 km/h (142 mph)— originally 222 km/h (138 mph)
Acceleration	0–100 km/h (62 mph) 7.4 sec (sports gearbox) or 9 sec (automatic)
Fuel consumption	10.6 litres/100 km (26.6 mpg)
Number built	Approx 35,000 6-series coupés of all types between 1976 and June 1982

Bosch fuel injection for those durable in-line sixes, but the 3.2-litre 745i had a single KKK turbocharger to provide BMW's most powerful current production engine (only the limited production M1 had more power) with 252 bhp and 36 Nm (265 lbf. ft) torque. The 745 designation refers to the engine capacity multiplied by 1.4, which is the factor used in international motor racing to classify turbocharged cars. It was certainly true that the 745i with its automatic transmission performed like many 4.5-litre cars, rushing to 'over 220 km/h' (137 mph) and reaching 100 km/h (62 mph) in 'less than 8.0

BELOW *Rather than produce the prototype V8 or V12 engines BMW had experimented with in the 1970s, the company chose to turbocharge the 7-series to produce the 745i model with over 250 bhp and 225 km/h (140 mph) capability. Equally extraordinary is the BMW 'four-cylinder' HQ building at Munich, shown left.*

seconds' in the justifiably proud words of its manufacturer. The 745i was never exported to Britain and the 218 bhp 735i was left to head the UK range in lavish extra equipment trim.

In general, the 7-series typifies the current BMW approach. Rather more conservative and comfortable than before, with the emphasis on every electronic aid to engine efficiency (including, on the larger BMWs, a fuel supply cut-off that operates on the overrun), yet with the same basic independent suspension layout under the skin. Like those marvellous six-cylinder engines the suspension, braking (many models now offer the ABS anti-locking system) and steering have been continuously revised over the years, with the result that the BMWs of the 1980s have kept up with the higher standards demanded by customers. Yet BMW still retains that elusive image that comes through the joyful driving character of the road cars coupled with a constant sports programme.

The future

BMW has largely met the most challenging automobile regulations in the world by ensuring that Americans can buy at least one example from each of the current line. For the 1982 season there was the fuel-injected 1.8-litre 320; the new high efficiency, low revving Eta 2.7-litre six for the BMW 528e; and the 733i and the 633 CSi shared emission control, 181 bhp versions of the faithful 3210 cc six. BMW's American horizons also stretched to provide Ford with examples of the M60 diesel engine the company produced with Steyr in Austria from 1983. Current offerings include a 518i—fuel injected from 1984—and there is also a new 535i with a 3.5-litre single overhead camshaft engine.

The company's sports activities have always allowed its customers a foretaste of the future, so it is fitting to conclude by completing the BMW motor sport story.

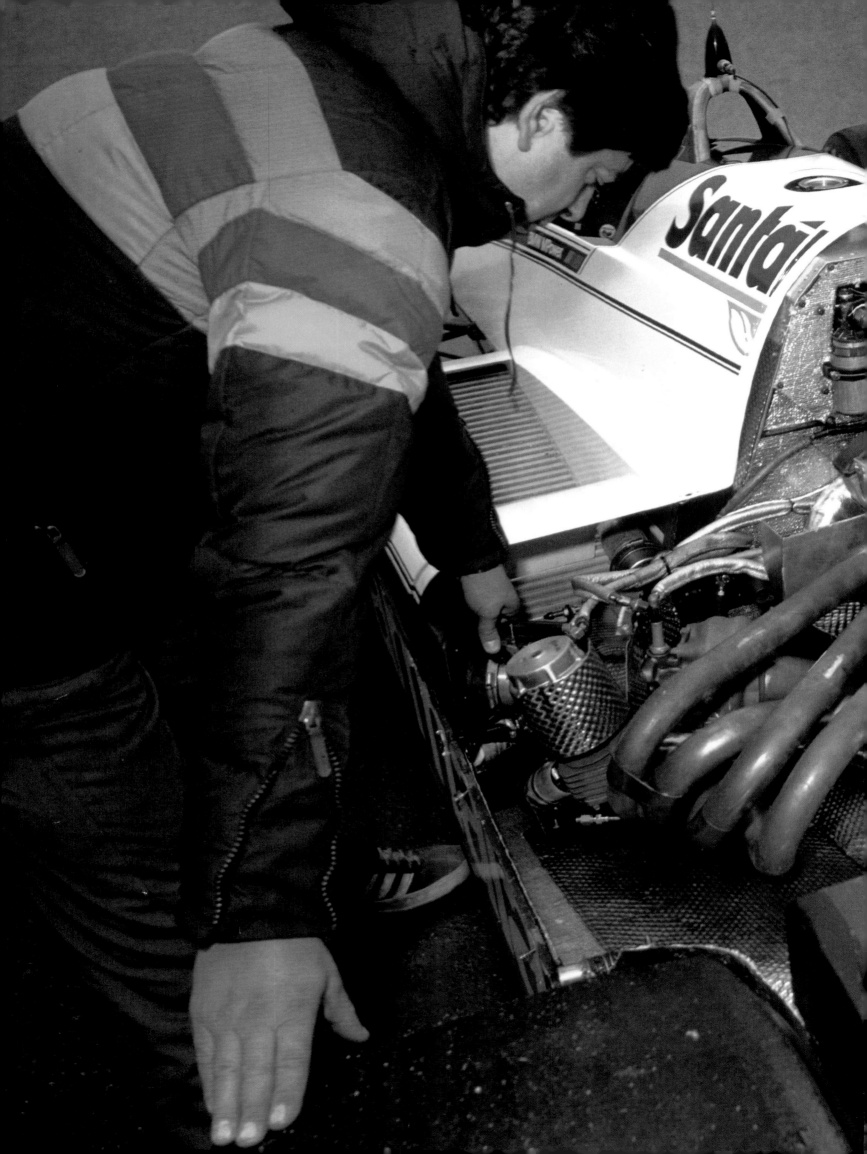

THE MOTOR SPORT PROFESSIONALS

In spring 1972 Jochen Neerpasch, former Porsche factory sports car racer and competition director for Ford in Cologne, took up his appointment at BMW: directing a new separate company within the Munich factory complex. Called BMW Motorsport GmbH, the enterprise would have the substantial backing of the parent company in endeavouring to wrest the European Touring Car Championship from Ford's team of Capris. It was also given the task of securing the European Formula 2 Championship, using a 2-litre version of the successful 16-valve engine developed before BMW's official withdrawal from the sport in 1971. All this was to be achieved in the following season, so BMW was back in an official racing capacity after a break of less than two years.

It could be argued that BMW was never really absent. After that official withdrawal some of the key competitions personnel, including engine man Paul Rosche and Alex von Falkenhausen, supported what they called BMW 'underground racing' from a small lock-up in the Munich suburbs! The results, employing Dieter Quester (von Falkenhausen's son-in-law), a March chassis and BMW four-cylinder engines, were spectacularly good in both the 1971 European Formula 2 Championship for 1600 cc cars and a similiar series for sports cars held the following year. In the latter the engine was run in 2-litre 16-valve form, and thus provided a good indication of its competition strength for the 1973 Formula 2 Championship, which catered for 2-litre engines.

The arrival of Neerpasch and Martin Braungart, his respected Capri chassis engineer wizard (also from the Cologne-based Ford team), ensured that this racing effort yielded even greater results in 1973. A link with March Engineering at Bicester in England was officially cemented: BMW agreed to supply its M12/6 racing 2-litre engine to a team of red March 732s that would be driven by Jean-Pierre Beltoise and Jean-Pierre Jarier. Additional finance would come from STP and the production BMW iron-blocked engines would be expected to provide 275 bhp at a resounding 8500 rpm.

However, the major challenge, as the German public and spectators all over Europe witnessed, was to take the weighty but powerful 3.0 CSL racing saloons to victory over the Ford team that Neerpasch and Braungart had only just left! To help them in this cause they took Hans Joachim Stuck Jnr from Ford as well and paired him with the unlucky but exceptionally fast Grand Prix driver Chris Amon from New Zealand. Of course Stuck's father had done great things for BMW in the past, as well as for the prewar Auto Union GP team, so this was a move that caught the public imagination, particularly as the young Stuck had such a spectacular driving style. A second striped works CSL for the 1973 season (which included outings at sports car races such as Le Mans and the Nürburgring 1000 km) was provided for the Dutch 1970 European Champion Toine Hezemans and Quester. While Ford lined up a spectacular array of Capri guest drivers—including Jody Scheckter, Emerson Fittipaldi and Jackie Stewart—BMW often held the advantages both in numbers and saloon driving skill, for Alpina fielded CSL BMWs for the likes of Niki Lauda, Brian Muir and Derek Bell. Fellow Bavarians and preparation specialists Schnitzer (four brothers, headed by engine expert Josef Schnitzer) also had their own CSL. Like Alpina, the team was encouraged by enormous cash incentives from BMW, so Schnitzer usually had a car out to take on the two or three Capris that Ford entered in an effort to score a hat-trick of victories in the European series.

The wings have it

That historic 1973 Ford vs BMW saloon car season began with the two sides fairly evenly matched. In March Niki Lauda and Brian Muir won the opening event at Monza, North Italy, in the orange Alpina BMW. The faster factory Fords and BMWs wilted under the strain of matching the reliable 202.87 km/h (126.06 mph) pace established

PRECEDING PAGES *The BMW four-cylinder engine celebrated more than 20 years' production with some astonishing performances in the 1982 Brabham BT50. Here the engine, winner of one 1982 GP, is prepared for 1983. Car provided by Motor Racing Developments.*

RIGHT *The larger photo shows the exciting development of the CSL coupé for American IMSA events; with its 450 bhp engine and modified body, it proved very competitive in 1975–6. The inset is the 1973 European Championship CSL described in the data panel.*

70

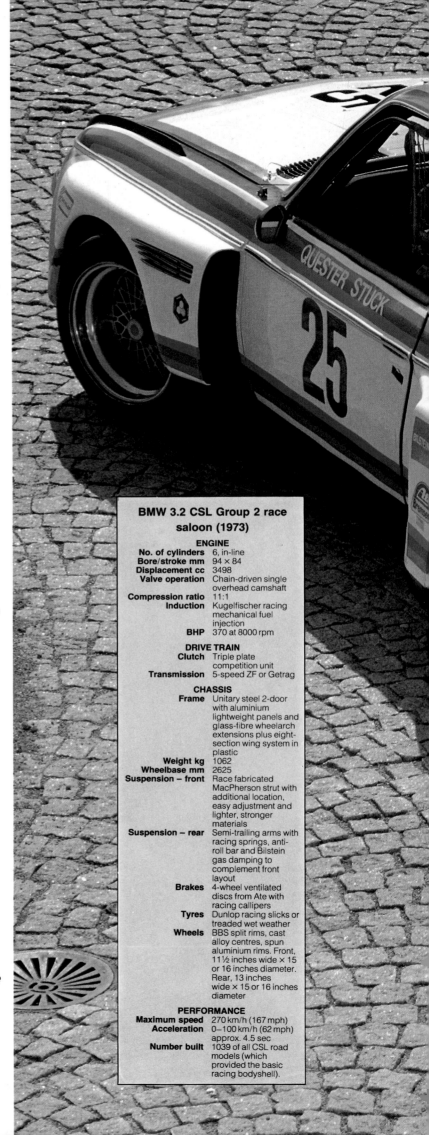

BMW 3.2 CSL Group 2 race saloon (1973)

ENGINE

No. of cylinders	6, in-line
Bore/stroke mm	94 × 84
Displacement cc	3498
Valve operation	Chain-driven single overhead camshaft
Compression ratio	11:1
Induction	Kugelfischer racing mechanical fuel injection
BHP	370 at 8000 rpm

DRIVE TRAIN

Clutch	Triple plate competition unit
Transmission	5-speed ZF or Getrag

CHASSIS

Frame	Unitary steel 2-door with aluminium lightweight panels and glass-fibre wheelarch extensions plus eight-section wing system in plastic
Weight kg	1062
Wheelbase mm	2625
Suspension – front	Race fabricated MacPherson strut with additional location, easy adjustment and lighter, stronger materials
Suspension – rear	Semi-trailing arms with racing springs, anti-roll bar and Bilstein gas damping to complement front layout
Brakes	4-wheel ventilated discs from Ate with racing callipers
Tyres	Dunlop racing slicks or treaded wet weather
Wheels	BBS split rims, cast alloy centres, spun aluminium rims. Front, 11½ inches wide × 15 or 16 inches diameter. Rear, 13 inches wide × 15 or 16 inches diameter

PERFORMANCE

Maximum speed	270 km/h (167 mph)
Acceleration	0–100 km/h (62 mph) approx. 4.5 sec
Number built	1039 of all CSL road models (which provided the basic racing bodyshell).

ABOVE *June 1975 and the BMW-versus-Ford contest continues in the German national championship race at the Norisring. Hans Stuck is in the front row BMW, Jochen Mass in the Ford. Both men led the event in a hectic battle, but Stuck retired on this occasion—he lacked the water-cooled brakes of his rival!*

by the Alpina CSL over 4 hours and 816.5 km (507.35 miles). The fastest lap was shared between the two camps, Jackie Stewart's 3.0 Capri RS 2600 and Vittorio Brambilla's Schnitzer BMW roaring around the parkland circuit at an average speed of 208 km/h (130.69 mph).

Because of bad weather the next European Championship round of 1973 was delayed until the Austrian Salzburgring could be cleared of snow. Ford won that round in May and the June event at Mantorp Park in Sweden, but BMW had been beating Ford in their battles within the German and world long-distance championship races held in between these European saloon car races. At Le Mans the 350 bhp, 3331 cc works CSL of Hezemans and Quester handsomely held off the Fords and surprised many with its 257 km/h (160 mph) pace along the Mulsanne straight. Besides winning the saloon car section of the classic *vingt-quatre heures*, the BMW was 11th overall.

The watershed for Ford and the beginning of total BMW domination in the European Championship came on 8 July 1973. Working at astonishing speed to prevent any Ford counter-move, BMW's Martin Braungart devised and had produced a complicated set of wings, spoilers and air dams that provided the big saloon with such tremendous stability that lap times around the hilly Nürburgring track dropped by nearly 15 seconds. This enormous margin was established with the 3.3-litre racing engine, but by the Nürburgring 6-hour race on 8 July, Paul Rosche's engine team had added a 94 × 84 mm bore and stroke derivative of the racing Kugelfischer injected straight six. From 3498 cc and an 11:1 compression ratio they extracted 'a lot more torque than before' and 370 bhp as the big six revved heartily to 8000 rpm.

The new 3.5-litre racing sixes were used to demoralize Ford in practice, with Lauda and Stuck seconds clear of Jochen Mass in the fastest Capri. Reverting to 3.3 litres for the actual race Stuck and Amon won for Munich at an average of 158.4 km/h (98.4 mph), which was a higher speed than the lap record a Capri had established a year earlier. BMW also found that the wings gave the cars astonishing cornering consistency so that they could run tyres with softer compounds and more grip than before. This led to an amazing Nürburgring run from Lauda who repeated his lap times to a tenth of a second for three tours of the crowded race track: the Austrian (then driving for the British BRM Grand Prix team) also established a new Nürburgring record at nearly 164 km/h (102 mph) average.

Ford did not win any of the remaining four European Touring Car Championship events of 1973, BMW taking the manufacturers' title by a crushing 6–2 score. And Hezemans won the drivers' title as well. The crowds, from Silverstone in Britain to the super-fast Spa-Francorchamps public road circuit in Belgium—where the winning BMW *averaged* 192.62 km/h (119.6 mph) for 24 hours!—could feast on their memories of the sliding, wheels-airborne, motoring they had witnessed as Ford fought to get back on terms. For 1974 both Ford and BMW planned a return bout, Ford this time equipped with the tail spoiler for the Capri RS3100 and over 400 bhp from a Cosworth 3.4-

litre variant of Ford's V6. Paul Rosche and his men were not idle in Munich either: they had a four-valve-per-cylinder version of the BMW 3.5-litre six producing 405 to 420 bhp by September 1973, ready for winter testing—and 1974.

Formula 2

Meanwhile, how did the BMW-March alliance shape up in Formula 2? Tremendously, in a word. In fact the results were so good that year, and for every racing season since, that March-BMWs were still racing and winning the European Championship more than ten years after the alliance was formed. During that period the iron block fours, progressively developed from that M12/6 into the 1974 M12/7 specification still used to this day, battled against purpose-built V6s from Honda, Renault and Ferrari, plus the all-alloy Brian Hart 420R racing unit that went on to become the basis of the first Toleman Formula 1 turbo engine.

BMW engines did not win every time against these opponents, but they always gave a good account of themselves despite an apparent power deficiency by the 1980s. That inaugural 1973 season saw Jarier win eight times and finish second twice to take the European Formula 2 title easily from the Ford Cosworth-powered Surtees cars of Jochen Mass and Patrick Depailler.

Since then over 300 BMW Formula 2 engines have been built and the company has won the European title seven times: 1973, '74, '75 (a Schnitzer-developed engine with BMW block), and 1978, '79, '82 and '83. The winning drivers for BMW were Jarier, fellow Frenchmen Patrick Dapailler and Jacques Laffite, Italian Bruno Giacomelli, Swiss Marc Surer, Italian Corrado Fabi and Austrian Dieter Quester, who

won in 1983. In most of these championship wins the chassis were provided by March as part of that loyal alliance, the exception coming from Martini in France for 1975. The BMW engine has won about half the championship races it contested since the 1973 début, which is a competition record to be proud of. By 1982, the engine was developing 315 bhp or more and was capable of withstanding 10,000 rpm. With Michelin tyres on the March chassis, Fabi and Johnny Cecotto scored eight wins. By 1984 engine output rose to 330 bhp.

In action the crisp sound of the fuel-injected M12/7 is totally different to the whooshing, flamethrowing performance of the Brabham-BMW Formula 1 four-cylinder unit. Yet, as so often with BMW, the common principles are evident. The gear-driven twin overhead camshafts, the provision of four valves per cylinder and the use of aluminium for the cylinder head and a production iron base for the cylinder block are the evident links with a tough Formula 2 engine that has made a superb basis for Formula 1.

Fuel crisis: survival

All those 1974 racing plans laid by Ford and BMW were severely bruised by the fuel crisis. In Germany the public were made very sharply aware of their fuel sources after the Arab-Israeli conflicts, and it was almost embarrassing to go racing at a time when many car factories were laying off workers. That BMW Motorsport survived at all owed a great deal to its marketing skills—anything from complete engines to handsome but high-priced sports wear—while the parent company had enough to do launching economy versions of some models.

LEFT *The 1973 March 732-BMW was a straightforward alliance between BMW's M12/7 racing engine and a good chassis design; its nimble 275 bhp brought it the 1973 European title.*

ABOVE *Jean-Pierre Jarier (seen here at the Pau street circuit in France) scored most March-BMW wins in 1973, with eight victories going his way. The March-BMW combination, plus Michelin tyres, continued in the 1980s, beating Honda-powered Ralt and Team Spirit V6s for the 1982 European Formula 2 Championship title.*

ABOVE *This beautifully presented Jägermeister BMW 320i (seen at Zolder in Belgium) was typical of the 300 bhp racing version of the 320i that the factory designed for the 1977 season. They were very reliable, cornered superbly, but needed more power.*

LEFT *The first 1974 confrontation between Ford and BMW, with both sides equipped with new engines providing over 400 bhp and speeds of 275 km/h (170 mph) plus, came at the spring Salzburgring event in Austria, in the European Touring Car Championship. Hans Stuck and Jacky Ickx drove the winning BMW.*

Yet BMW did pursue a motor sport programme throughout the 1970s. The 24-valve M49 engine was used in 430 bhp guise for the second round of the 1974 European Touring Car Championship at Salzburgring and duly won in the hands of Stuck and Ickx at an average 188.35 km/h (116.9 mph). Resplendent in new midnight blue colours the factory CSLs also raced at the Nürburgring round in July, but failed to finish. Further appearances in anything but the German national series were precluded by finance.

In 1975, following the BMW takeover of the American concession after a protracted legal battle with the previous privately owned management, it was decided to re-establish the name Bayerische Motoren Werke in the public eye by sending Stuck and suitably modified CSLs to appear in American events. This they did with success, spending 1976 with former Porsche Champion Peter Gregg. Then they switched to McLaren North America and the BMW 320 as a racing base, gathering much useful turbocharging information for the four-cylinder. The turbocharged 320i made its début at Road Atlanta in 1977, with driver David Hobbs of Britain at the wheel, and it won four races that season.

During the 1976 World Endurance Racing Championship series BMW also raced highly modified Group 5 CSLs capable of more than 470 bhp, with a potential 1000 bhp in turbocharged 3.2-litre trim. BMW ran Porsche very close in the title hunt because of the reliability exhibited by the 290 km/h (170 mph) normally aspirated CSLs. The rarely raced turbocharged CSL of 1976 was the most powerful competition BMW ever built, a daunting sight with Swede Ronnie Peterson at the wheel, even though no one dared boost it to more than 800 bhp—and even then this 298 km/h (185 mph) monster was not able to finish a race.

BMW recovered its confidence and amazed German spectators with a three-car team of lightweight Formula 2-engined 320i saloons for the 1977 Deutsche Rennmeisterschaft (German Racing Championship). The BMW 'Junior Team' comprised young hopefuls Eddie Cheever, Marc Surer and Manfred Winkelhock, all of whom

BMW M1 road car (1979–81)

ENGINE

No. of cylinders	6, in-line; mid-engine location
Bore/stroke mm	93.4 × 84
Displacement cc	3453
Valve operation	Chain-driven double overhead camshafts, 4 valves per cylinder
Compression ratio	9:1
Induction	Kugelfischer-Bosch mechanical fuel injection; 46 mm chokes
BHP	277 at 6500 rpm
Torque	330 Nm (243 lbf. ft) at 5000 rpm

DRIVE TRAIN

Clutch	Fichtel & Sachs, twin plates, hydraulic operation
Transmission	Rear mounted 5-speed ZF transaxle with final drive to halfshafts and rear wheels

CHASSIS

Frame	Tubular steel stressed chassis and 2-door unstressed glass-fibre body
Weight kg	1300
Wheelbase mm	2560
Track – front mm	1550
Track – rear mm	1576
Suspension – front	Double A-arms, coil springs, 23 mm anti-roll bar, Bilstein gas dampers
Suspension – rear	As above but 19 mm anti-roll bar. Ride height adjustment front and rear
Brakes	4-wheel disc brakes, ventilated with power assistance, rear pressure limiter. Front, 300 mm diameter, rear, 297 mm diameter.
Tyre size – front	205/55 VR 16
Tyre size – rear	225/50 VR 16
Wheels	Cast alloy; front, 7 inches wide; rear, 8 inches wide. Both 16 inches diameter

PERFORMANCE

Maximum speed	261 km/h (162 mph)
Acceleration	0–100 km/h (62 mph) in 5.6 sec
Fuel consumption	19.6 litres/100 km (14.4 mpg)
Number built	Approx 450

later went on to Formula 1, but their intense rivalry often led to car-damaging bumping and scraping. Although this was highly entertaining for the crowd, BMW preferred to appoint Hans Stuck and Ronnie Peterson to tackle the task of racing in a rather more gentlemanly manner when the youngsters were briefly suspended.

The factory's experiences with turbocharging the 320 racer were fairly disastrous, but they did assist Schnitzer toward some German championship success with a 1.4-litre 320 turbo. This developed up to 380 bhp in 1978, when it took journalist and racing driver Harald Ertl to the German national title against fierce Ford-Zakspeed opposition.

M1: a blind alley

Unable to gain board support to go into Grand Prix racing, Jochen Neerpasch steered BMW Motorsport into the most expensive sports car racing and construction programme ever. The vehicle was the M1, a mid-engine cocktail of the BMW 24-valve engine with Italian glass-fibre style and separate steel chassis (only 450 were produced, including a 277 bhp road-going version). This device was intended to be turbocharged and wrest the endurance title from Porsche, but it lagged so far behind schedule that Neerpasch and the Formula One Constructors Association (FOCA) eventually cooperated with Goodyear backing to put on two years of the best-rewarded and fastest single-make racing ever seen. In 1979 and 1980 many of the GP drivers competed in the ProCar series for M1s; Niki Lauda and Nelson Piquet emerged as well-paid champions. You could say Piquet's alliance with BMW began at that stage, for he also drove an M1 to a fine third overall with Hans Stuck in the Nürburgring 1000 km in May 1980, its best world sports car championship result.

All this expenditure and delay on the M1 programme, plus the sheer bother of producing more than 400 road cars to satisfy international sporting rules, made the BMW board restive. It may be suspected that these men jumped at the chance of selling Talbot a Formula 1 turbocharged version of BMW's rugged four-cylinder racing engine. The suggestion was made by Neerpasch, and Germany's most famous postwar competitions director left BMW in November 1979 to join Talbot, hoping to advance that 1.5-litre racing programme from France.

PRECEDING PAGES *The larger photo shows the fabulous spectacle that BMW M1 one-marque racing made as a supporting event to European Grands Prix. This is from 1979, when Niki Lauda won the ProCar series for M1 racers; in 1980 it was Nelson Piquet's turn.*

PRECEDING PAGES, INSET *The BMW M1 road car to which the data panel refers.* Autocar *magazine tested one example in 1980 and found it had a 262 km/h (163 mph) maximum, and needed just 5.5 seconds to sweep from rest to 100 km/h (62 mph).*

ABOVE *In a year of rapidly changing fortunes, Nelson Piquet persisted with the BMW-powered version of the Gordon Murray-designed Brabham GP car. Here he collects his reward with this June 1982 victory in the Canadian Grand Prix at Montreal. The powerful and compact BMW Turbo and the agile Brabham chassis were modified for 1983 into BT52 form, with revised rear suspension, and engine developments covering the electronic ignition and exhaust.*

LEFT *The Schnitzer brothers have prepared BMWs for years since Josef Schnitzer's German national championship win in a 1966 2000 TI. Even Josef's death in 1978 did not sever the links, as this 1979 M1 for Sepp Manhalter showed.*

Brabham-BMW BT50
(1982)

ENGINE		DRIVE TRAIN			
No. of cylinders	4, in-line	Clutch	AP Borg & Beck racing	Tyre size – front	24-inch diameter × 11 inch wide Goodyear
Bore/stroke mm	89.2 × 60	Transmission	Rear Hewland FG 400 transaxle with 5 or 6 forward gears	Tyre size – rear	26-inch diameter × 15 inch wide Goodyear
Displacement cc	1499			Wheels	Brabham. Front 13-inch diameter × 11 inch wide or 15 × 11. Rear, cast magnesium 13 × 16 or 15 × 16
Valve operation	Spur gear-driven twin overhead camshafts; 4 valves per cylinder	**CHASSIS**			
Compression ratio	Approx. 6.7:1	Frame	Monocoque		
Induction	Bosch-Kugelfischer mechanical fuel injection; KKK twin flow turbocharger and intercooler	Weight kg	590 (unballasted)	**PERFORMANCE**	
		Wheelbase mm	2768	Maximum speed	Up to 327 km/h (203 mph)
		Track – front mm	1752	Fuel consumption	62.77 litres/100 km (4.5 mpg)
BHP	From 570 bhp at 9500 rpm	Track – rear mm	1600	Number built	6
Torque	From 442 Nm (325 lbf. ft) at 8500 rpm	Suspension	Double wishbones, pull rods operating semi-inboard front springs. Koni dampers		
		Brakes	Girling and AP 4-wheel ventilated discs; sometimes Hitco carbon discs and pads		

Politics, heartbreak and victory

It was the Austrian former editor of the Swiss weekly *Powerslide*, Dieter Stappert, a BMW competitions administrator from 1977, who got Neerpasch's job. Stappert knew that his first priority was to retain that Formula 1 engine for BMW's own use, for it would be the jewel in any sporting crown.

Stappert succeeded in convincing both his immediate superior, Hans Erdmann Schönbeck (BMW sales director since 1974), and the engineering chief appointed in 1975, Karlheinz Radermacher, that the 1.5-litre Turbo F1 engine should be for BMW's use in a chassis of the company's choice, with possible commercial sales to follow.

By February 1980 Paul Rosche and his team of 20 men were able to use the newly constructed BMW Motorsport department at Preussenstrasse to the full extent. It had marvellous facilities above and below ground (including four Schenk-equipped engine test cells monitored by TV), and serious work began on the F1 engine. On 8 March 1980 Stappert met Brabham and FOCA chief Bernard Ecclestone to lay the groundwork for an agreement that would see Brabham designer Gordon Murray adapt the already successful BT49 to accept the BMW turbo. Murray asked for a slight reduction in the weight of the production block—BMW managed approximately 4.5 kg (10 lb) and found that well-used old 1500 cc production blocks were the best basis for F1 engine construction. The BMW unit also had to be laid out with its ancillaries to clear the vital ground effect paths on the Brabham chassis.

By 13 October 1980 (Stappert's 38th birthday) the engine was ready for its first running trials at Silverstone. Further development at Paul Ricard and other race tracks, plus constant work in Munich on aspects like the electronic engine injection and ignition systems, provided such a basis for optimism that the car was allowed to compete in public practice on 17 July 1981 at the British GP. The fast Silverstone track suited it—and the regular Brabham BMW driver Piquet—admirably and they recorded the third fastest time. The BMW's race début came on 23 January 1982 in the South African GP, but neither of the now purpose-built BT50s finished, Piquet crashing early on in the race.

Victory came in the fifth event in which the Brabham-BMWs had been entered and astounded everyone, for the previous weekend the team had plumbed the depths of racing misery by failing even to qualify to race in Detroit. Just seven days later, on 12 June 1982, the 1499 cc KKK-turbocharged Bayerische Motoren Werke's Grand Prix engine won the Canadian GP in Montreal. Fittingly, the driver was Nelson Piquet and he was supported in second place by Riccardo Patrese, his Brabham BT49D Ford Cosworth V8 team mate.

It had not been easy for either Brabham or BMW, especially while they tried to achieve race-winning reliability in the middle of the season—always a desperately difficult task. But by mid-season the combination had emerged as one of the most formidable in the GP world. Indeed in 1983 Nelson Piquet won the world championship in his Brabham BMW: a superb triumph for the Munich company.

INDEX

Acknowledgements

The publishers would like to thank the following individuals and organizations for their kind permission to reproduce the photographs in this book:

Special photography: Ian Dawson 1–5, 22, 26, 32, 33, 37, 38, 40, 41, 52–3, 56–7, 60–1, 62; Rainer Schlegelmilch 8, 9, 11, 12, 13, 16–17, 18–19, 20–1, 23, 24, 25, 27, 28, 29, 30, 31, 34, 35, 36, 39, 42, 43, 44, 47, 49, 50, 58, 59, 62–3, 65, 66, 67, 70, 71, 73.

Autosport 51; BMW 6–7, 44–5, 46, 47, 64–5; Ian Dawson 77; LAT 48, 51, 73, 79; Rainer Schlegelmilch Endpapers, 63, 71, 72, 74, 75, 78.

In addition, the publishers would like to thank Klaus Wesner, Johannes Schultz and Richard Gerstner at BMW AG (public relations); Olaf von Gostkowski and Hans Fleischmann at BMW AG (archives); and Raymond Playfoot and Michèle Cory at BMW (GB) Ltd. They would also like to thank the BMW Car Club of Great Britain, especially Peter Samuelson, the Secretary, and Wolfgang Marx of the International Council of BMW Clubs for their help and assistance. The publishers would also like to thank BMW AG for giving them permission to photograph the cars in the BMW museum at Munich. Finally thanks are due to the owners of the other cars who kindly allowed their vehicles to be photographed.